Expat
TEENS TALK

Peers, Parents and Professionals
offer support, advice and solutions
in response to Expat Life challenges
as shared by Expat Teens

Dr. Lisa Pittman and Diana Smit

First Published Great Britain 2012

by Summertime Publishing

byexpatteens.forexpatteens@yahoo.com.sg
www.expatteenstalk.blogspot.com
www.expatteens.org

ISBN: 978-1-904881-53-7

Cover and interior photos and cover concept by Claudia Bennett, Expat Teen, IB student, Singapore

Book design by Graham Booth - Creationbooth.com

DISCLAIMER

The information contained within this document has been altered to protect the identity of the individuals who provided it. Any perceived similarities between the information within and any individual's experience should be considered to be coincidental.

Dedications

Diana's Dedication

I am dedicating this book to my three teenagers because they, like me, recognize and support the need for *Expat Teens Talk* – a book to help and advise Expat Teens, worldwide, in times of need, providing the tools for how to deal with situations that are sometimes too challenging to manage all alone. I would also like to dedicate this book to Peter, my loving and very supportive husband, who believed in this project from the beginning. Thank you for your support and encouragement throughout the journey of this project.

Dr. Lisa's Dedication

I dedicate this book to my family and friends, who have provided me with support in ways that nobody else could. In addition, it is because of my interactions with my clients – both in a monocultural setting, as well as an international setting – that I have been able to become the well-rounded professional that I am today. So, I want to dedicate this book to all of those Expat Teenagers out there who have been (unknowingly) waiting for a resource like this to come out. I truly hope that this book provides you with the support that you need and/ or allows you to take a deep breath and say, "I'm glad I'm not the only one..."

Praise

"I think this is a great new resource for expat teens and fills a gap in the resource market for this unique population. I have recently become an expat myself and as an adult this transition poses a number of challenges that really only other expats can understand. Whilst the move is exciting, the challenges are real and can be quite isolating and I can only imagine that these challenges are multiplied for expat teenagers, who often have little say in the moves and changes that they are facing. The teenage years are a time when a stable peer group and 'fitting in' are paramount and the expat experience can cause havoc in these areas, along with a range of other obstacles the teen has to face when moving to a different country.

I like the fact that this book goes right to the target audience and sources real questions and answers from the teens who are currently experiencing the expat lifestyle. The issues are relevant to those teens going through this experience now; they are not what adults or professionals think are the important issues to teens. The teens, adults and professionals who answer the questions give first-hand and practical tips for dealing with the issues raised by the teens, rather than abstract concepts or ideals. The authors have done a great job in recognising the need for such a publication, researching the issue, collecting responses and questionnaires and putting it together in a readable and usable format for all those involved in the life of the Expat Teen. This book will hopefully help the teens find the good and wonderful experiences involved in this lifestyle, while helping them navigate some of the more difficult times they may go through on this journey."

Bronwyn Towart, B.Ed, M.Ed MAPS
Psychologist working with teenagers in Australia

"*Expat Teens Talk* really is a great approach to deliver guidance in this manner and teens will find it easy to accept and relate to. I am absolutely convinced that this book is raising concerns, and providing direction, for questions that many teenagers are facing. The format of giving guidance from three different points of view is unique and very credible, and the teenager can take what he or she wants to from the responses. The book in fact has its relevance not just for Expat Teenagers, but for any teenager struggling to cope with moving from one community to another, or even one school to another."

Tim Nettleton, Geneva, Switzerland
Works for a major educational organization; is the father of three daughters who each hold three passports and live a completely bilingual life.

"Wow! It's really good to emphasize the 'pick up and read' aspect of the book – that it's not to be read from cover to cover, but as related to difficulties or questions [an Expat Teen may have] … as is natural, some of the answers of the peers, parents, and professionals are similar. I love the little blurbs throughout ('Expat Teens say') and the information at the end (related to statistics and resources and the mind map) is really, really great! I find the direct links in the comments helpful and timely for the reader. Great work!"

Sharon Racine, Geneva, Switzerland
Advisor – Roots4Legacy, Crossing Cultures

"My goodness, I am impressed! You ladies have come up with a great concept, which has translated into a great book. It's refreshing to have teens themselves expressing their concerns, triumphs and advice. The one-line quotes, in particular, were spot on. As I was reading I had a few moments of déjà vu! I've been an expat for most of my life, as a child, a teen, and a mother of three expat children, now all grown up. I've lived firsthand the numerous challenges, joys and heartbreaks my teens went through, and I know how important a good support system can be. This book certainly provides a lot of encouragement.

"*Expat Teens Talk* really is a great approach to deliver guidance in this manner and teens will find it easy to accept and relate to. I am absolutely convinced that this book is raising concerns, and providing direction, for questions that many teenagers are facing. The format of giving guidance from three different points of view is unique and very credible, and the teenager can take what he or she wants to from the responses. The book in fact has its relevance not just for Expat Teenagers, but for any teenager struggling to cope with moving from one community to another, or even one school to another."

Tim Nettleton, Geneva, Switzerland
Works for a major educational organization; is the father of three daughters who each hold three passports and live a completely bilingual life.

"Wow! It's really good to emphasize the 'pick up and read' aspect of the book – that it's not to be read from cover to cover, but as related to difficulties or questions [an Expat Teen may have] … as is natural, some of the answers of the peers, parents, and professionals are similar. I love the little blurbs throughout ('Expat Teens say') and the information at the end (related to statistics and resources and the mind map) is really, really great! I find the direct links in the comments helpful and timely for the reader. Great work!"

Sharon Racine, Geneva, Switzerland
Advisor – Roots4Legacy, Crossing Cultures

"My goodness, I am impressed! You ladies have come up with a great concept, which has translated into a great book. It's refreshing to have teens themselves expressing their concerns, triumphs and advice. The one-line quotes, in particular, were spot on. As I was reading I had a few moments of déjà vu! I've been an expat for most of my life, as a child, a teen, and a mother of three expat children, now all grown up. I've lived firsthand the numerous challenges, joys and heartbreaks my teens went through, and I know how important a good support system can be. This book certainly provides a lot of encouragement.

I wish it had been available a few years ago. It goes a long way to reconfirm that expat life is sometimes a hardship, sometimes a gift, but always an adventure!"

Michelle S., Dubai
Mother of three Expat Teens

"*Expat Teens Talk* is a much-needed resource for the millions of teenagers trying to make sense of the mobile world we live in. The book is full of experiences that are authentic, emotive, powerful and relevant. However, this book is much more than just a range of experiences; the advice and strategies provided by teens themselves, parents and professionals is timely, accurate and realistic. Congratulations Lisa and Diana for developing a resource that gives internationally mobile teens hope and understanding about their world."

Ian Moody
Head of Counselling, United World College of South East Asia, Singapore

----

"This is a must read for all teens, parents and the increasing number of leaders who are growing businesses through developing and growing people around the world.

As the father of three citizens of the world who were born in Switzerland to parents who are American and British, and who have lived in France, Switzerland, Hong Kong, Sweden, the UK and the USA, I find the insights shared and the advice contained in the book compelling.

As a business leader who has been instrumental in growing businesses and people in over 140 countries, I have seen, firsthand, the benefits of international experience in this increasingly frontier-free world. Moving associates and their families is a game-changing event; it can grow associates and their families immensely. It can also be one of the most stressful, frightening and, sometimes, disastrous experiences lived. The book accurately and deeply addresses the issues faced and provides compelling advice on how to reach the highs and avoid the lows of expat life.

As an expat father, husband and business leader who also cannot answer simply the question "where are you from?", [if] this book had been written 30 years ago – [it] would have helped me immeasurably. Without it I guess that I muddled through – and we all had fun doing so."

Peter R. Hempstead,
Procter & Gamble, 1976–1999; six country moves
Wm. Wrigley, Jr. Company, 1999–2008; one home (Chicago); business in 140+ countries
SVP International and SVP Global Strategy and New Business

Thank you

We would like to thank all of the people who have helped us bring this book to life:

- Participants from the focus group discussions.

- Participants from the Peer, Parent and Professional feedback sessions.

- Schools, worldwide, that allowed us to have access to their students, and promoted our project to their Expat Teen populations.

- Our mentor, Ruth E. Van Reken, for her ongoing support and encouragement.

- Diana and Dr. Lisa thank each other for being on the same wavelength throughout.

- Our respective families, friends and support systems.

- All Expat Teens and Expat Teen Alumni who shared their stories with us for publication.

- All of the Expat Teens that we work with (and are raising) and that inspired us to take on this project.

Foreword

by Ruth E. Van Reken

Co-author *Third Culture Kids: Growing Up Among Worlds*

Wow! What a great book you are about to read! These stories, written *by* some of you Expat Teens *for* the others of you, will help you realize that this global journey you are on, with all its joys and challenges, is not a lonely one. There are many who share your basic story of moving between and among different cultural worlds during the years when you are trying to understand who you are and where you do or don't fit in this world.

In seeing what you share with others, you will also discover what is distinctive about your personal story. Seeing both the commonalities of your story and the distinctions is important. When we don't understand what we share with others, or when we don't fit a particular traditional model of cultural or ethnic identity that others expect us to be, we can easily wonder what is 'wrong'? When we don't understand our uniqueness as being this particular person called 'me', we have a harder time finding the areas of life where who we are – with our particular personality, natural talents, and skill sets acquired through the experiences of our lives – make a perfect fit.

This is a book that I wish I could have read when I was a teen. After living the first thirteen years of my life in Nigeria – the land of my birth – I returned to what my passport declared as 'home' for me – the USA. With one airplane ride, all the ways of life I knew as 'normal' disappeared. No longer could I bargain in the market for the best price on my bananas. I waited for the inevitable crash during simple drives to the store as I watched cars race at us – all from the wrong side of the road! My skills at soccer had no use in a land that called a seemingly silly game with players running with the ball in their *hands* 'football'. I, who had been so full of confidence and joy in one place, suddenly wondered why I could never seem to do life 'right' in this next place. Knowing that the smirking classmates who watched me while whispering to one another were, in fact, mocking me for such ignorance sent me home in silent tears each day. Why didn't they like me? What was I doing wrong? Why couldn't I 'get it' like everyone else? I felt incredibly alone during that transition.

I can only imagine how much it would have helped me at that time to read the stories that you are about to read. Instead of blaming myself for being "so stupid," I would have learned that the experience of trying to find a way to 'live well' in a new culture is common among internationally mobile teens – whether we are repatriating, as I was, or going to a new place overseas. And, besides learning that what I felt was 'normal' for my experience, I could have read (as you are about to do) tips for how to navigate these sometimes turbulent waters more successfully. I had no idea when I was a teen that some of the stresses that I felt could be turned into some of my greatest assets to live well in a globalizing world if I learned strategies for not only surviving, but growing as a person through these times of change.

That's why this book is so important.

For many years, Dr. Lisa Pittman (a practicing psychologist) and Diana Smit (an educational therapist) have used both their professional expertise and personal expatriate experience to try and help teens who are living the same kind of expat experience you are. As these women listened to your peers, they realized that they were hearing many common themes from these teens, no matter which country they came from or which specific countries they had lived in. Yet, when Dr. Lisa and Diana wanted to offer resources to help these Expat Teens deal well with the common challenges that come up, they couldn't find any book written just for you. They found books that gave advice on how your parents and teachers could help you, but they wanted something that you could read and use for yourself.

And so this book was born.

This is not a book in which others write *about* you, but in which other Expat Teens simply tell their *own* stories. In each one, you will likely find places where you connect to the feelings they express, and understand what happens when you grow up in an internationally mobile childhood. You will also see details which are not identical to your life story and give you better insight into the places where your story has its own unique thread.

An added bonus, however, is that after reflecting on your experience through the lens of other Expat Teens, you will discover that this book is about more than simply identifying common feelings. Following each story are concrete ideas from fellow Expat Teens, Expat Parents, and Expat Professionals on how you can turn even the challenges into rich places of growth. My deepest hope is that all of you Expat Teens who read these stories and the practical wisdom included in the pages ahead will discover what I did from my own journey – that the enormous wealth gained from a globally mobile childhood can be one of your greatest assets in the days ahead – for you, for your family, and for the world that you will one day be leading.

Ruth E. Van Reken

Table of Contents

PART 2 – The Authors Respond.....................133

Chapter Six: Dealing with trauma

Chapter Seven: What happens after Expat Teen life

Chapter Eight Alumni reflections

Who is this book for?

Expat Teens "Talk"

This book is for Expat Teens, Expat Parents, and Professionals working with Expat Teens in Expat communities: international school teachers, international school counselors, international school principals, and outside professionals (i.e. doctors and psychologists).

The idea for this book developed when Diana and Dr. Lisa's searches for a book directed at the needs of Expat Teens proved futile. To date, the majority of Expatriate/Third Culture Kids/Global Nomad publications are directed at Parents and Professionals. There is no resource (book, manual or self-help guide) that we could find that was specifically targeted to the needs and different challenges that Expat Teens face throughout their lives (in particular, their adolescent years), nor is there a resource that enables them to learn more and understand that most of what they are going through and what they feel as a result of constant change in their lives is 'normal' and shared by many other Expat Teens worldwide.

We decided that the most valid way to fill this void in available resources was to create one ourselves. As Professionals in our respective fields, we are in contact with Expat Teens daily. As a result of the sensitive nature of our professional relationships with Expat Teens, we often find ourselves in the role of 'confidante' and learn a lot about the challenges Expat Teens are confronted with every time they move from one country to the next, which generally results in many changes, such as schools and social groups.

Being a teenager is not easy – it is a time of abundant life changes (internal and external) – that inevitably make them question who they are. The years of adolescence are transformative years of growth and development that bridge childhood and adulthood, and are considered to be the most sensitive and challenging years in one's lifetime. Going through the teenage years as an Expat, having a transient lifestyle of change, makes these years doubly challenging.

So, what did we do about it? We first thought about writing a book to Expat Teens to let them know that what they are feeling (frustration, fear, anxiety, wanting to escape, and so on) is normal, especially considering that they do not have constants in their lives (for example, a constant social group to grow up with, or constant exposure to a wider support network of extended family, family friends, teachers, neighbours, who have known them for their entire life). After further thought and discussion, we realized that going to the Expat Teens themselves, as the experts, would be a way to meet the need, providing teen-to-teen support.

In keeping with the global perspective of and interest in our objective, we reached out to as many Expat Teens as we could access. We contacted International Schools, Embassies, relocation agencies, and community groups in Expat communities worldwide. We developed a website (www.expatteens.org) and invited Expat Teens, worldwide, to share with us their stories, questions, challenges, fears, and experiences. In return for their submissions, we provided them with support, advice, and solutions – the tools needed to deal with what they were sharing.

Instead of providing the 'Dr. Lisa Pittman and Diana Smit point of view', we went to the 'experts' on a broader scale. We had feedback sessions with diverse groups of Expat Teens, Expat Parents and Expat Professionals. The model we came up with reflects these three voices, providing a broad perspective of solutions, advice and support.

We realised early on when embarking upon this project that many Expat Teens struggle to confide in their peers (this is especially difficult when you just move and do not yet have an established peer group). Many Expat Teens do not have a communicative relationship with their own parents and are reluctant to talk openly and share what they are going through as a result. We also, most importantly, realised that most Expat Teens do not know the role of Professionals – psychologists, psychiatrists, counsellors – and therefore do not necessarily access them when needed. In addition, most Expat Teens do not know who the Professionals are in their respective Expat communities. If they do, they often do not have the financial means to access these services for support, independent of their parents. We therefore decided that it was critically important to include all three perspectives in our feedback. Expat Teens need to hear what these three very important groups have to say in support of their shared stories.

How to use this book

How Expat Teens can use this book

We feel that you, the Expat Teen, will be able to relate to the submissions that were selected for publication, i.e. similar story, different details. Therefore, the Peer, Parent and Professional responses will be relevant and helpful in terms of supporting your understanding about how to deal with what you are going through. This is meant to be a 'dip in, dip out' book, one that does not have to be read from cover to cover.

Read through the submissions as sent to us by Expat Teens worldwide. Ask yourself: How do I relate to this? How do I feel about it? How do I deal with it? Read the feedback and reflect on how you can apply it to your own situation. We have provided space for you to note your 'reflections' after each submission. We hope to provide the tools and information that you need to empower yourself and other Expat Teens worldwide.

How Expat Parents can use this book

As parents we cannot always be expected to have all the answers. Parenting is a challenge; ensuring the well-being needs of our children are met and supporting them in developing into independent, confident young adults is not always easy. Who do we turn to when we do not have the answers? Who do we go to for parenting support when confronted by something we do not know how to deal with? Where do we turn when we find ourselves feeling challenged by the same things our children feel challenged by?

Expat Teens Talk is full of support, advice and solutions from Expat Parents, people who are going through the same experiences as you, raising Expat Teens in countries other than their own. This book will support you, the Expat Parent, in understanding some of the challenges Expat Life presents your children. More importantly, it will help you understand and support your own child with the challenges they may be going through as a result of having a life full of constant change.

How Expat Professionals can use this book

As an Expat Professional (for example, psychologist, counsellor, teacher, school administrator, member of clergy), you come into contact with Expat Teenagers on a regular basis. Many of the situations that these teenagers encounter may not come to your attention, which may leave you wondering about their overall well-being. Chances are, many of them are adjusting well and are able to deal with situations that arise. However, it is likely that there are some students who are not handling things well and, for one reason or another, do not seek assistance to help them cope.

We encourage you to read through these submissions as sent to us by Expat Teens worldwide. Ask yourself: How would I respond to this if a student came to me with this situation? Is our school/community/place of worship set up to handle similar situations? What can I do to let our student body/youth group know of the resources that are available (including myself) in this area/region/school/place of worship? We have provided space for you to note your 'reflections' after each submission. We hope to provide tools and information that will help you identify some of the issues facing Expat Teens today and to further assist you in establishing yourself as a viable *known* resource for your Expat Teen population.

Questionnaires

Before inviting Expat Teens to write to us to share their experiences and stories, we did a lot of research via questionnaires. The purpose of this was to validate the need for the resource we had in mind. We had the strong impression that these Expat Teens shared with us things that they had never shared with anyone before. There are Expat Teens out there who really need support. A sample of our questionnaire is provided in the appendix. Feel free to access our website (www. expatteens.org) to send us a completed questionnaire or to share your Expat Teen story for our next publication.

Confidentiality and Anonymity

We assured all Expat Teens who shared their stories that all submissions chosen for publication would be anonymous and confidential. We did not ask for names, addresses or contact details. We provided the platform for Expat Teens to share openly, with full confidence that it was okay and safe to share their stories.

All submissions have been edited (as clearly stated on our website) to ensure that the writer remains anonymous. There are no names, gender or indication of age. Some stories have been split into separate submissions in order to clearly address one issue at a time and provide clear feedback accordingly. In addition, the quotations that are included at the end of each section were obtained from Expat Teens and are included, without credit, in an effort to maintain anonymity.

The individuals who contributed to this book are truly multicultural. In order to maintain the integrity of the information that we received (i.e. in order to 'keep it real'), we have left the responses in the 'voice' of the person(s) who provided the information. Therefore, you will see throughout the book different spellings for similar words, phrases that may be culture-specific, and other nuances – the combination of which you may not find in other books.

Please note that these are not errors – they are a true reflection of who our audience is: the Global Citizen who can read between the lines and still understand the lesson. In other words, this book is for YOU!

Introduction

Life as an Expatriate (Expat) can be fascinating. Expats are individuals who live outside of their passport country and are exposed to a lot of change, including: new Host Countries each time they move, new schools, new language(s), new culture(s), new people, new houses, new friends – in many respects, a new life. Expat Life is a life full of discovery, newness and, often, a lot of travel. However, as exciting as change can be, it can also be challenging and difficult.

Around the world, in many Expat Communities, there are outlets of support for stay-at-home partners through Host Country Embassy welcome events, International Clubs, coffee mornings, and interest groups. For the Expat Professional, there is often a human resources individual who can provide support and answers to new challenges as a result of an international move... but, what happens when an Expat Teen has a problem, an issue, a question, a fear, or an experience that he or she finds difficult to deal with on his or her own? What happens when an Expat Teen feels that he/she cannot discuss his/her problem at home, or at school with a teacher or counsellor? What if the issue/problem/challenge that the Expat Teen is struggling with is too personal to share with parents, an employer, school, or new friends? Who can an Expat Teen go to in any and every Expat environment, whether to share sensitive issues and concerns related to problems at home (separation/divorce, excess parental travelling, communication issues), or a problem with peers, relationship difficulties, cultural differences, issues with drinking and drugs, a problem/concern/fear related to sex, an STD, pregnancy, or date rape? Who do these Expat Teens have to confide in with full confidence that their story will remain confidential?

We, Dr. Lisa Pittman and Diana Smit, have discovered that there are needs that are not being met in expat communities worldwide: the specific needs of Expat Teens. Through professional and personal experiences with Expat Teens living in different Host Countries around the world, we have found that when an Expat Teen has an issue, challenge, fear, question, or experience needing support, in many settings there are no (obvious) support systems, and often, teenagers do not know how to access the support systems that are in place. Local, Host Country community access or social services, for example, are often out of reach as a result of cultural, religious, or language barriers. In addition, in schools (international or local) where school counsellors are employed, they admittedly do not have specific training to deal with serious personal, family, or mental health related issues. Many times, Expat Teens have little access on a day-to-day basis with their extended families and friends left behind (on a previous assignment or in their home country). Finally, external professional help is either difficult to find or unaffordable if Expat Teens are unable to share their problems with their own parents. So, who do they go to?

This book aims to be a resource that Expat Teens can use to access the advice, solutions and support for problems, challenges and issues they are confronted with or struggling with as a result of their Expat lives. The stories shared may not be identical to every Expat Teen's personal experience, but the hope is that Expat Teens worldwide will be able to indirectly relate to the experiences and stories shared and, subsequently, benefit from the support, advice and solutions provided by three critically important and influential groups in their time of need: Peers, Parents and Professionals.

We hope that you are able to benefit from this book and we welcome feedback at byexpatteens.forexpatteens@yahoo.com.sg.

PART 1
Peer, Parent and
Professional Feedback

CHAPTER ONE:
Ambivalence about moving/Expat Life

'On the road – AGAIN!'

"*I am an Expat Teen who has lived in my current country (which is not my home/birth/passport country) for most of my life. I basically consider myself to be an 'adopted' local. However, my parents have recently announced that we are moving. I've always wanted to live in a country with four seasons and now it is going to happen. I know that this is a great opportunity for me to live in a country that I have never lived in, and I know that it will be very different from where I am now. However, I'm not so sure that I want to move to a new city, a place that has all four seasons and a totally different culture. Things I worry about with this move include academics, safety, and friendships. For me, since I am in the first year of a two-year high school program, it is quite an inconvenient time for moving and I'm nervous. In the new city, I will be attending a different international school system that has a different academic program. I've never heard of this teaching system and I'm hoping that it will be easy for me to adapt to a new learning system. I'm also worried about the fact that my new city isn't as safe as my current city, so of course I'm scared – it will be a whole new environment. I'm going to miss my friends, and also the amazing food! The weird thing is that I've met so many great people here and I am extremely upset that I have to leave soon. Overall, I hope that moving to the new city will make me realize how lucky I am to be travelling around so often and meeting new people. I am hoping that I will come back to my current city so that I can revisit all my friends.*"

PEER Responses

Keep in touch with old friends

- Stay in contact with friends you 'leave behind' – stay in their lives.

- Keep in mind your previous friendships – you will always need access to people you know and trust, another person to talk to and confide in.

- If you struggle with making new friends, talk to your old friends about what they would do.

Keep a positive outlook about the experience

- Appreciate new experiences.

- All you can continue to do is learn from this adventure.

- Try and expose yourself to the new surroundings/culture.

- It is an adventure – be positive/optimistic!

- You will make friends. It may take time, but don't worry!

- You are very lucky to be able to travel so easily – it is very rare.

- This does not mean 'goodbye'… with your ability to travel, revisiting your friends will be a possibility.

How to address the safety concerns

- Go out with friends until you are comfortable – be cautious/careful, make yourself knowledgeable about the 'safe and unsafe' things to do in your new city, and don't go out alone until you are okay about safety. But try not to worry about it too much.

- Talk to your parents, as they have probably considered all of this as well. Plus, they may have a better idea and may be more knowledgeable about the new place than you are.

How to deal with the academic issues

- Academics will work themselves out.

- Most International Schools have programs for students in the middle of a two-year course.

- Your parents will have thought about this as well, so trust them.

- When in school, make sure to socialize so you can learn how people interact and spend their time.

- Presumably, if you were accepted into the new school, then they are prepared to support your academic needs to help you transition into a new academic program.

- Always try hard, academic wise – it's always encouraging to get good grades.

- Work hard to ensure you can cope with the new school system.

Go to people for support (family, friends)

- Friends, teachers, and counselors will all help with the transition.

- Make sure to keep your family in this adventure – they will always be a good source of help.

- Talk to your siblings about moving.

What you are going through is normal – find others who have been through the same thing

- It is absolutely normal to feel this way! Believe it or not, there are so many other Expat Teens who have done the same thing.

- It's okay to worry – use that to help you.

- A lot of the things that you mentioned are going to surprise you when you move. If you keep an open mind, then things like friendships, culture, and food will be easier than you think.

- Seasons are great to be exposed to, as is culture and, if anything, you can learn a lot from them.

- Moving is always hard.

- Embrace the culture.

- You will adapt – do not worry about the differences.

- Try and make the most of the new city.

- Remember: you are going from one international school to another international school. Teachers and students alike are used to change and supporting others through change, so you will be fine – trust the system.

PARENT Responses

Do you have any choice or say in the decisions?

- Have you clarified for yourself what you want and need? Have you expressed this to your parents? Perhaps by voicing your needs and concerns, they will be able to support you in learning more about the academic changes, and help you maintain strong ties with your current school and friends – even create opportunities for you to return to visit.

Think about the role of change

- Your attitude and expression of how you perceive this upcoming change are very mature and positive. You are going through normal, healthy and balanced feelings that are typical for an Expat Teen facing change of this kind.

- The timing is clearly not ideal, as you are in the middle of a two-year academic programme. Communicating how you feel with your parents, friends and school is very important. There are likely to be others in your expat environment who have experienced similar change and these people can support you.

- Remind yourself that there are always positive and negative aspects to change – it is good to appreciate both.

- You have clearly thought through the impacts of change and how you feel about it, which is admirable. Look forward to enjoying the four-season climate that you will experience. Look forward to the new foods, people, habits, and environment. Stay in touch with your current environment through communication with friends (for example via Skype, Facebook and email). Learn recipes that you can reproduce in your new environment, and keep doors open to be able to plan and enjoy a return visit when you are ready. You have the right, balanced attitude, and you are a realist – good for you!

Consider the impact of international schools midway through an academic (two-year) programme

- Is there an option of boarding at your current school to enable you to complete your programme?

- Can you get academic support from your current school and new school to help facilitate the transition? How can you best be supported to make this as easy as possible?

Communicate

- Talk to friends, teachers, and/or your counselor at school. Find people who have experienced a similar change, especially those who have moved during a two-year academic programme, and learn from them the best ways of dealing with academic change. Ask how to maintain old relationships, while at the same time developing new ones in your new school and surrounding environment. Expat Teens in your current country have also experienced change. Find out how they can help and support your needs related to your upcoming change.

PROFESSIONAL Responses

Find ways to transition and adapt

- The things that you describe are similar to what a person who is leaving 'home' for the first time might describe. Recognize that this is a normal feeling and it takes time to get used to the idea of moving, even after you have moved. Moving could be considered a loss and the conflicting feelings are part of the grieving process.

- Safety is something that is relative, no matter where you live. You always have to get used to one place being more or less safe than the previous place. Try not to dwell on this too much and just make sure that you do what you need to in order to keep safe.

- A part of you is excited to move to a country with four seasons, while another part of you is unsure about learning a new system. Embrace both parts and figure out how to manage the feelings associated with each one. It's okay to feel conflicted about this, as it is a normal part of the transition process.

Educate yourself about the new place

- Do some research about your new city so that you can have some knowledge about it before you go and can maybe have something to look forward to when you arrive.

- Be proactive about exploring your new city! Try to find things that are similar to your previous place(s) of residence, as well as things that are unique to your new place of residence.

- Learn more about the new academic system that you are going to be part of. Try to focus on similarities to your current system, and identify who you can go to if you have questions about the system. Taking these steps is important, both before you move and after you arrive.

- Try to talk to the curriculum coordinator about the academic program and/or ask to be able to communicate with a same-aged peer who can answer your questions about what it is like to be a student in that school/program.

- Take advantage of opportunities to visit the new city before you move. Ask to visit the school that you will be attending, especially if they are in session, so that you can see how things work first hand.

- If you can't visit the city/country/school beforehand, seek out students in your current school who may have lived in that city/country before and ask them about their experiences. Also, if you live in a place where there are other schools that follow the academic program that you are about to move to, ask around to see if you can talk to a student from that school so you can get an idea of what to expect (e.g., if you are currently in an IB program but are moving to an American system, find out if any of your friends know of anyone at the American School in your current country whom you could talk to about what the American system is like).

Get closure

- Third Culture Kid literature talks about 'building a RAFT': **R**econciliation, **A**ffirmation, **F**arewells, and **T**hink destination (David C. Pollock and Ruth E. Van Reken in *Third Culture Kids: Growing Up Among Worlds*, 2009). Keep these things in mind, and try to find ways to say 'goodbye' to your current city and say 'hello' to your new city.

- Celebrate that you have had a chance to be in the city that you are about to leave, and also celebrate the opportunity to move to a climate that you've always wanted to experience.

- It is really important for you to maintain friendships in the place that you are leaving, as this will help you with closure.

Focus on positive aspects of transition

- Try to focus on some of the opportunities that you will have as a result of moving to a place that you've always wanted to move to, including some of the doors that will open for you.

- If you are successful in your current city, then you will probably be successful in your next city. Trust in yourself to be able to make the transition a positive one.

- Think of this move as practice for your future – it sounds like you may be heading off to university soon and the things that you are currently experiencing may be similar to what you experience when you go away to university. Use this as a time to start practicing your independence.

Use school as a resource

- School can usually be a good place to turn to for safety and resources. Brainstorm with other friends/peers about safe places where you can spend time.

- Participate in school programs that will allow you to meet new people, as well as get to learn the school system.

- Take advantage of being in a school system where there are other Expat Teens and use that opportunity to share your experiences and learn from others.

- It is important to orient yourself as much as you can to your new school. Take advantage of orientation programs and other transition programs that are geared towards helping students settle into their new surroundings.

Keep in touch with friends

- While it is important to meet new people, it is also important to keep in touch with your old friends. History could repeat itself and you could find yourself having opportunities to meet similar people in ways that you never imagined.

Expat Teens say...

"Being an Expat Teen means you have more than one home."

PERSONAL REFLECTIONS

'There's no place like home?'

"Being an Expat Teen for me has its advantages and disadvantages, but so does life in general and I find that, for me personally, being an Expat Teen is very rewarding. Having never lived in my 'home country' my whole life, answering the question 'where is home?' is hard. Is 'home' where you feel most comfortable? Is 'home' where your parents and family are from, if they are even from the same place? Is 'home' where you live now? In the end, I find myself having several 'homes', all answering the previous questions. When in my 'home country' the place I live is 'home'. But when I am where I live for most of the year, the country where my extended family lives is 'home'. For the most part, I will just answer simply, if possible, or with the simplest answer depending on the situation. When I return to my 'home country' I try not to talk much about where I live or my expat life, since a lot of the time, I get the impression that they do not want to hear it. Where I am from, you are not supposed 'to be something', so people think I am bragging or trying to be better than them, which is not the case at all! This is one of the few things that may create a disadvantage when going off to college – I would not know where to fit in. This is why finding a university with an international status has become crucial to me. I do not know if I will fit in well, since it is not the same as starting at a new international school, where people are used to backgrounds like mine."

PEER Responses

Define 'home'

- Home is where the heart is.

- It is okay to have your own definition of 'home'. Think of yourself as lucky to have such a choice.

- Home can be many things – it is something that connects you to a country, city, people, and school. It is where you feel you belong; what you feel a part of because you relate and connect to it.

- The place where you currently live, where you invest your day-to-day time, where you are involved, where you know other people, where you belong in terms of school, sports, friends, family – this can be defined as home.

Be proud of having several homes

- Having several 'homes' is great! Be proud and think of how knowledgeable and flexible you are as an individual as a result.

- Having lived in various countries and experienced change and diversity has had a positive impact on you, making you more aware and sensitive to differences. As an international citizen, you have the life experience to fit in anywhere.

Don't be ashamed of who you are

- Do not be ashamed about being an Expat Teen! Embrace it, and the people who really matter in your life will know and understand that it is a part of who you are and that you are not bragging.

- People who ask you questions do so because they want to know more about you. Reward them by explaining about your multiple homes. Explain what that means, and how this has impacted your life and who you are. Develop their understanding.

- In today's global world, the color of your skin, your nationality, ethnicity, or geographic location, does not define WHO you are. Your personality, character, interests, like/dislikes, strengths, weaknesses, fears, emotions, and so on, make up WHO you are.

- Embrace that fact that you are 'different' – it makes you special and unique, and enables you to offer so much more to others around you.

Figure out what would work best for you regarding university

- Don't be intimidated by the future – stay true to yourself and you will be okay.

- Choose a university that suits your needs in terms of course of study, environment, and climate. Factor into consideration what you like and what makes you thrive and make decisions accordingly. Doing your research will enable you to make an informed decision.

- Do research on universities with high international student and international staff populations. These statistics are all published on university websites and in university prospectuses.

PARENT Responses

A short answer is a simple answer

- The shortest answer is most often the easiest, but as it is a starting point for what could be lasting and meaningful new relationships, especially when adapting to life at university, find an answer that validates your past without having to go into lengthy detail.

- Give the shortest answer you can to define where you are from. Think about your past and simplify your response. Those truly interested in developing relationships with you will learn, over time, about your past, but those will also be the individuals who are interested and who care.

- A simple answer such as "I am American/Bolivian/Indian, but grew up overseas" is often good enough. If people are truly interested in knowing more, then you have given them the opportunity to ask.

Don't worry about fitting in

- There are environments all over the world in which you will fit. Go and visit, look around and learn. Your Expat Teen life is full of advantages and it is really great that you acknowledge that.

- You already have the skill set to transition, adjust, and acclimate. Trust yourself and enjoy!

Look ahead to college/university transition

- Find yourself a copy of *The Global Nomad's Guide to University Transition* by Tina L. Quick. It is a wonderful, insightful guide on how to make the transition to university easier for Expat Teens.

- As an Expat Teen, you may find it easier to transition to university... you have been exposed to a life of change and adapting, so in your own right, you are already experienced.

- Treat your launch to college/university as you would a reassignment to a new country. Do not assume that everyone will be interested in your background, but make an effort to ask about theirs.

- Find activities that you enjoy and you will inevitably find like-minded friends. Work on building bonds on commonalities. Respect others and they will respect you. Be yourself!

- Recognize and accept that it is not always easy, but remind yourself that you already know that.

PROFESSIONAL Responses

Embrace your uniqueness and find common ground with your peers

- As you have said, your international experiences will undoubtedly make you feel different from most of the people you will be surrounded by on your college or university campus. You do not share common experiences of growing up with them. It is important to remember that, although you may feel like you don't fit in, it doesn't mean there is anything wrong with you.

- Your dilemma is a common one for Expat Teens. They can be perceived as being arrogant by simply trying to share their life stories. Sometimes it is necessary to downplay your experiences until people get to know you better. Instead of saying, "One time at the beach in Bali..." try simply stating, "One time at the beach...".

- You don't need to hide or forget parts of your life, but it may take time for others to be ready to hear about them. Try asking questions of your peers so that they might be interested in hearing about you in return. Start off simply, with questions like: Have you lived in the same place all your life? What is that like? Do you live close to your grandparents or other relatives? What is the farthest place you have ever traveled to? Where would you go if you could take a long trip? Eventually the questions will be directed towards you and you can share back without sounding haughty.

- Look for others with whom you may have some shared experience – other Expat Teens. You may find them amongst other international students. Think about starting an Expat Teen/ TCK club on your campus.

- There is a new resource available for Expat Youth who are making the transition to college or university in their home country or to another Host Country that addresses all the issues you have raised and more.

Expat Teens say...

"You know you're an Expat Teen when your answer to 'Where are you from?' is, 'I don't know.'"

PERSONAL REFLECTIONS

CHAPTER TWO:
Challenges of moving

'Same, same, but different'

"I have lived in four different countries in different parts of the world. When I was young, moving from country to country was easy; now that I am older, I find it much more challenging. When we left my home country to move to the one we currently live in, I found it very difficult because my entire life was in my home country. I had a great school, strong network of people, and good friends. I knew the place back to front. I am currently living in a different country surrounded by an unfamiliar language with new ways of doing things. Every day is a new experience in my life. Eventually, these new experiences will become part of my daily life. My experiences in the previous cities in which I lived, as well as the city where I currently live, are very different from my home country. But, it is a fact of my Expat Teen life that I will have to get used to seeing vast differences in the cities and countries that I live in. Learning how to do that is my challenge.

When we first moved to our current country of residence, everything was really hard. We didn't know where the basic things were, like the hairdressers or the supermarket. We knew absolutely no one here at all! Moving to a new school was the hardest of all. It took me many weeks of feeling frustrated and being upset, trying to fit in and settle down. At times, I genuinely thought I was depressed/suicidal because I felt so lost in a world that was so different from the one I knew. I felt that nothing that I tried to do was ever simple.

I used to be afraid of going to school because all of the people were so different – they didn't know me and I didn't know them. I think that this is one of the biggest problems about being an Expat Teen: you're at a time in your life when you really need close people around you, and often, these people live on the other side of the world. This makes a lot of situations very upsetting and hard to deal with. I have since learned that you need to give yourself time to get accustomed to your new life, and you should always expect some difficult and challenging experiences, as well as some good and positive ones."

PEER Responses

Find people with whom you have things in common

- Expose yourself (put yourself out there), take social initiative – for example, introduce yourself to students who are in more than two of your classes.

- There are always new students in international and in local schools as a result of moving, so there will always be a group of people that is similar to your old friends, and people that you find you have things in common with.

- Talk to some of the other new kids and see how they are adapting. This conversation could form a bond and possible friendship.

- Sports teams, art club, music group, and interest groups are good places to make friends.

Communicate

- Tell someone about your frustrations – your parents, family, a teacher or school counselor.

- Open up to the new people around you and try to be spontaneous – it usually helps.

- You can always talk to your family – they are going through the same thing you are. They might be a great source of stability and comfort and support.

Maintain relationships from the past

- Maintain your old friendships/keep in touch with old friends.

- Confide in an old friend, perhaps one from your old school, and just tell them about your troubles and frustrations. Ask how they would react and what they would do.

- Take with you those lessons that you've learned from previous assignments.

Know that what you are going through is normal!

- No one likes change.

- I agree that it is very difficult, especially not knowing where anything is. But once I established a couple of friends, I found that everything else all of a sudden fell into place. I was lucky in that I got along really well with a couple of the new Expat Kids, and we helped each other out.

- It is true: teenage life is the hardest time to move. You are not alone – many other teens (Expat Teens and non-Expat Teens) have been through your situation.

Take time, be patient

- New environments can be scary, but are not the end of the world. Change can be a good thing and if things don't get better and you don't feel at home living around the world, you will know this when you are older. At that point, you should consider living in your home country.

- If you struggle to make friends, take some time and find your feet. Life isn't a rush – you'll find your place! You are not alone!

- It takes time to fit in. Don't worry!

- Valuable lessons are learned through moving – communication, respect for other cultures, adaptation.

- Take the first month to sit back, observe your surroundings, and find where you want to make your mark at the school.

- You will get used to it. In time, things will become easier. Be friendly, be nice. However slow it is, these things tend to work out.

Be positive, enjoy the change, and maximize your opportunities

- Stay positive/optimistic!

- You can adapt – these new experiences becoming a part of you do not mean your old ones are getting erased.

- You will get used to this – there are worse situations (like terrorism, violence, corruption).

- Parents are normally the first ones to go looking for other expats, so don't be shy to ask them about any possible friendship opportunities for you.

- It's great that you're finding the positive – it's important to be optimistic about a move and new experiences.

- Enjoy the difference! One day, you will be able to tell good stories about it.

- The differences are only a part of life – if every place were the same, life would be boring!

Expose yourself to the culture

- Buy some guidebooks so that you can find out about your new country before you move. This will help with the process of change, as you will arrive more prepared and knowledgeable.

- You should try to explore the new city, preferably with new friends.

- Use the opportunities you are given to try a new food, or to witness a cultural or religious event that you otherwise wouldn't be able to see.

- Try to learn the basics of the local language – it will help make adapting easier.

- Different languages and cultures expose you to the world and new things – enjoy it while it lasts.

PARENT Responses

Be positive and mature

- You are to be complimented on your mature and positive attitude! It is great that you are aware of the impact of your experiences, but also open to new ideas.

- Be proud of where you've come from, yet cognizant of 'experiences' that are different from your home country, or other countries you have lived in.

- Change and diversity can be, and often are, positive – embrace them!

- You clearly see opportunities and challenges in needing and wanting to adapt to change, as opposed to focusing on difficulties and impediments. Keep up your positive attitude, and try to remain balanced, rational and sensible. You will succeed with your honest attitude.

Be ready for, and mindful of, the long-term impact of this experience

- It is evident that you recognize and identify the challenges of your changing lifestyle. Expat Life is challenging, but you are not alone in experiencing and adapting to change. Find others around you – at school, within your immediate family – and discuss the changes you are going through. Being open and talking about it will expose you to the feelings and coping strategies of others, which you will benefit from. You too can contribute ideas and suggestions to others, as you are clearly aware of the changes that you are exposed to as a result of your Expat Lifestyle.

Participate in culture and other groups

- Peers with similar backgrounds can provide you with support. Join a sports or cultural activity group at school to bond with like-minded peers and share experiences.

- Find out if your home country or previous country of residence has any teen, support, or cultural groups that you can join to maintain a connection with the previous city you have lived in and/or your home country.

- There are peers in your expat environment who can relate to your experiences of change. You can be your own 'change agent' but recognize you are unique.

PROFESSIONAL Responses

Transition and orient yourself

- It seems you have hope about being able to get used to the 'vast differences', which is a good starting point!

- Continue to embrace the differences and explore them even further as they become part of your regular experiences.

- Change can be difficult, but it appears that you have a positive outlook, which will help you adapt.

- Consider reading books about local culture; learn about your new environment and all it has to offer.

- Seek out opportunities to integrate with local families to learn the culture and to share your culture.

- You may not have a full understanding or awareness of what 'home' is and may feel like a 'Global Nomad' as time progresses. So celebrate where you come from (i.e. the last school, or country in which you lived) by doing a class presentation, talking to friends, and so on.

- Expose yourself to cultural events, mother tongue classes, arts, and foods within your new culture.

- Consider participating in a sport or other activity that will allow you to meet other individuals from the local culture and/or from other cultures.

- Talk with your school about whether or not they have a 'buddy system,' which would pair you up with a current student. This could help make your transition a bit smoother and you could ask your 'buddy' questions that you may not feel comfortable asking an adult.

- Keep a record of the people and places that you have visited and use your knowledge of those experiences to interact with new people.

- Celebrate new ways to do 'old' things (for example, eating with chopsticks versus eating with your hands versus eating with a knife and fork).

- Be patient with yourself! Give yourself enough time to adjust, and have realistic expectations about how long that will take and what you hope to learn in the process.

- Surround yourself with as many support people as you can, including your family (both those who live with you and those who live in other countries) and friends.

Reconcile old experiences with new experiences

- Use your positive outlook to find ways to understand your new environment so that it can live side-by-side with what you experienced in the other cities in which you lived and vice versa.

- When you compare your new culture with your old cultures, look at the differences as 'interesting' and not as 'wrong'.

- As you keep track of the experiences you have, identify for yourself how joyful experiences translate from place to place.

Focus on similarities

- Try to look for similarities between your new culture and your old one – make your new experience your own without comparing it too much to your previous experiences (at first).

- There may be some cultural similarities and skills that you can transfer from your previous place of residence to your current place of residence.

- Look for similarities within school systems or settings, as the uniformity of academic programs may be comforting during a process that can be described as chaotic at times (e.g., if you were in an IB program in your previous country, being immersed in new school with the IB program will be a process that is familiar).

Communicate

- Consider finding someone else from your previous country, your current country, some other country (particularly if they are going through or have gone through similar transition issues), or a mentor with whom you can talk about what you are going through.

- Schools could create an open forum during which students can discuss such challenges.

- Peer groups could be formed to promote sharing of similar transition issues. They could be coordinated with new students only, or could be a mixture of new students and current students.

- Schools could have an orientation for students and families who are new to the country.

- Keep in touch with friends and family back 'home' (however you define 'home') or in your previous place(s) of residence.

Expat Teens say...

"Life is always interesting... an adventure is always around the corner."

PERSONAL REFLECTIONS

'Going local'

"I went from an expat international life to a local life. I like where I live; however I wish that other Expat Teens lived where I do. My biggest issue in this local environment is loneliness. I feel very isolated from the people around me. Although I have friends in my neighborhood, they seem like superficial friends because we don't think or believe alike – we do not really have a lot in common. I miss having friends who are more like me, other expat friends who relate to my expat experience. I feel that other Expat Teens would relate to discussions about things, like what we want from life, what is good and not good for us, and stuff like that. I miss having 'like-minded' Expat Teen friends."

PEER Responses

Adapt

- Open up, walk in the shoes of those around you for a while and see things from their perspective. Things may not be the same, but there are opportunities for you to grow and learn in your new environment. Put aside your differences and focus on what you have in common with others in your new environment.

- Find people with similar interests – such as music or sports – to develop entries into new and interesting friendships. At school, where you are surrounded by people the same age, working towards similar academic objectives is the right environment to find someone you can relate to and work on developing a new friendship with. You need to surround yourself with people who are interested and care in order to get the support you need to adapt to this new life.

- Having new people around you will ensure there are always new things to talk about. This will enhance your spectrum of people and show you more about their lives. Locals will have long-lasting stable relationships; this is an opportunity for you to work towards developing longer, deeper relationships. Try to get to know them. You will be surprised by how similar they are to you, not necessarily in terms of history and life exposure, but in terms of day-to-day interests, hobbies, points of view, and sense of fun. Broaden your own horizons and work on adapting.

- Realize that there is unity in diversity.

- Be patient and be friendly.

Seek family support

- Talk to your family – you may find that they are experiencing similar challenges and having similar thoughts and feelings.

- Seek advice and support from your family and the counseling staff at school – there are people around you who can help.

Find opportunities to learn and discover

- Things may not be the same, but this is an opportunity to learn. Learn about how your friends feel about not having had any opportunities to move around and experience change. Learn from them how to adapt and live in a single cultural environment with like-minded people surrounding you. If you close up and keep everything inside about how you feel, it will only get harder to settle.

- As an Expat Teen, you immediately have something that distinguishes you from the others, which you can use to your advantage. If you and the others around you don't think alike, then take this opportunity to bring something different to the table. The others around you may enjoy and appreciate you sharing your experiences and perspective. Don't underestimate what you may be doing for them through exposure and sharing.

Keep in touch with old friends

- Keep in touch with your old 'like-minded' Expat Teen friends and share how you feel. Expat Teens are experts when it comes to dealing with change. Don't underestimate how they can help and support you.

PARENT Responses

Give the locals a chance, get to know them

- Rather than focusing on the differences between you and your new peers, take the time to learn about what you may have in common. Focus on specific interests – sports, music, art – and inevitably you will find an entry point of common interests on which you can work towards building new relationships.

- The local kids will actually have a lot in common with you once you have the opportunity to get to know them – much more than you would ever imagine at the beginning of a new situation in a new peer group. They may not share all of your views or interests or sense of humour but they will share some aspects.

- Find out what the local cultural 'norms' are. The more you learn about your new peers, the easier it will be to determine a natural entry point to work towards developing new relationships.

- Finding others with an interest like yours will be of HUGE benefit! Finding a common sporting interest, for example, is very helpful in breaking down the cultural barriers.

Seek support of friends and family

- Maintain relationships with your 'like-minded' expat friends. They will understand what you are going through as a result of adapting to change, and they will be able to empathize and offer support and advice.

- Open up the discussion and share how you feel with your friends and family. Ask them about their past experiences and find out what they would do if they were 'walking in your shoes'.

Balance your expectations

- We often set ourselves up for disappointment when we set too high expectations. Try and look at your situation for what it is. What makes the new people around you interesting? What would you like to know and learn about them? What is important to you in regard to friendship? What do you want/need in a friend? What can you offer as a friend yourself? Take a step back from making comparisons and try and see your new surroundings and peers from a more neutral and open-minded perspective.

- Your new 'local' situation may never be the same as being surrounded by Expat peers, but it can be interesting and rewarding in different ways.

PROFESSIONAL Responses

Be aware of your assumptions

- Be careful about assuming that the peers around you cannot relate to you just because they have never been expats. Give them the benefit of the doubt.

- Are the people in your peer group really superficial, or are you using that as an excuse to not have to get to know them? Give them a chance.

Get involved in your current community

- This is a perfect opportunity for you to offer yourself to others, who may be very interested in where you are from, what your hobbies are, and so on – you may be surprised!

- Find activities that you used to do overseas and do them now. This will help you find ways to meet like-minded friends, and will also be a reminder of life overseas.

- Find new activities that you can do, and/or start a club or group at school, maybe even with people who live in your area (for example, neighborhood or apartment/condo), that focuses on international topics and issues. You may find more like-minded peers that way.

- Even though you are in your local community, there may be other international people who live in the area. As a result, they may have expat-type groups that you could be a part of, so try to seek them out. In addition, there may be schools or community clubs/centers that have a more international population, so consider seeking them out and seeing how you can get involved with their programs.

Keep in touch with your peers

- Keep in touch with your expat friends so that you can keep that connection to your life as an Expat.

- Does keeping in touch with your Expat Teen friends make it hard for you to fully embrace your current circumstances? It's important for you to find a way to balance the life you used to have with the one you currently have. Until you are able to move forward from your life as an Expat Teen, it will be difficult to feel fully a part of your current 'domestic life'.

- Talk to other Expat Peers who may be experiencing the same phenomenon (i.e. others who may have moved back to a 'home country') and find out how they managed the experience.

Get family support

- Talk with your parents about how they are dealing with the transition. If you have peers, talk to them as well and provide support for each other.

- Talk with your parents about the possibility of going back to visit one of the former countries where you lived.

Consider your mindset

- Adjust your mindset, especially if you are going to be living in this place for a while. Being negative about the experience could result in you missing out on some positive aspects of being in that setting.

- Depending on how old you are, consider going to university abroad or doing a year of study abroad. As you get older, you can always consider living overseas again.

Expat Teens say...

"Expat environments make you so used to being in a diverse community. Moving into monocultural environments is deceiving because you might actually be 'different' for the first time in your life."

PERSONAL REFLECTIONS

PEER Responses

Consult your family

- Talk to your family about this because they, too, may have or be experiencing similar feelings. Work through how to best deal with it together.

Seek out rituals and activities from faith

- Research and practice your own faith, with the aim to grow and develop as a believer. You do not need a support team to do this. Take initiative and indulge in your beliefs yourself, as this is important to you.

Be open to other faiths and their point of view

- Having been exposed to other religions, you should realize that not everyone is the same. Faith and beliefs should not hold you back from socializing and making new friends. Don't limit yourself and potential relationships with others by developing criteria for friendship. Be open-minded and get to know others, regardless of their faith. You can find like-minded believers through your church, religious institute, and religious mentors.

- Don't choose your friends based on their religious beliefs alone – give others a chance. Seek out others who share other like interests: sport, music, activities. Be open-minded and fulfill other friendship needs.

- Get to understand and appreciate other faiths. Learn what others go through to meet and balance their religious and social needs.

Talk to someone of the same faith

- Consult someone who 'believes' to discuss how you feel, and develop solutions in terms of how to find like-minded friends.

- Talk to your parents and teachers of faith.

- Find out from your religious circles how others seek out people of the same faith. There are other avenues besides school: church, mosque, temple, religious affiliated social groups, the internet, through family.

PARENT Responses

Practice your faith

- Find an outlet – a church, mosque, temple or other religious facility – where you can practice your faith and be surrounded by like believers. This will enable you to continue to grow, develop and feel empowered by your beliefs.

- Find a like-minded community, or create one. Perhaps there is something common to the different faiths that would be strong enough to hold an interest or allow one to grow even if it was different. Perhaps people of a different faith might have a similar base of priorities.

- What about starting a group that represents your faith and seeing through networking if there happen to be others living in the same city who share this faith?

Adapt your means of practicing and sharing your faith

- I guess the other side of the argument could be that if there *really* is nobody else of the same faith and the other religions are just too different, then this needs to be a part of your life that unfortunately cannot be shared right now except with friends or fellow worshippers, from other parts of the world, via social networks. You may find that you will have to decide to accept friends of a different faith and accept them on a different level so that you don't isolate yourself.

Look outward

- Identify your other strengths, interests, and passions to develop a social network and relationships. Try and identify other interesting qualities of the people around you on which you can work towards building and developing new and meaningful friendships.

PROFESSIONAL Responses

Don't make assumptions

- You are assuming that people who may not be part of your faith cannot be trustworthy or cannot hold you accountable. Be careful about making such assumptions, as that is not always the case.

- Networking is key. Ask around. There may be others just like you who are also looking (for an outlet for their faith).

Find a place of worship

- If you are able to find a church, synagogue, or mosque to practice your faith in whatever country you are in (even if the congregation meets in someone's home), you may be able to find an accountability partner there. You may not necessarily find someone of your same age, but if you end up interacting with someone older, chances are you will learn a lot and this person may turn out to be a wonderful mentor for you.

Maintain a support system

- Keep in touch with your former friends and/or members from your places of worship in other countries. They may be able to provide some support for you as you navigate your current environment.

- Talk with your parents (and siblings, if you have them) about how they are able to cope in this new environment, particularly if your faith/religion is not the dominant one in the country.

- If your religion/faith has related websites, they may also have blogs or chat rooms. Explore those resources and identify if you can get support in that way. If you can, then you can have that support no matter where you are in the world.

Expat Teens say...

"Keeping an open mind and having no expectations are qualities that would really make 'settling in' easier for Expat Teens."

PERSONAL REFLECTIONS

CHAPTER THREE:
Stress and worries about grades, school and appearance

'Worry, worry, worry'

"I don't have anyone to talk to and I feel alone. I'm going to tell you about things that I never tell anyone. I have too much to think about and I'm hurting people I don't intend or want to hurt. One second I'm so angry and the next I feel like crying.

I can't sleep at night because I can't stop worrying about things like school, grades, exams, homework, due dates, social stuff (like friends and boys), and trying not to make fun of myself. I also get worried about my friends telling other people about who I like, because that will lead to a week of teasing and embarrassment.

I also worry about presentations at school – my appearance, my weight – and then I make up plans about how to lose weight and am disappointed when they don't work.

I can't talk to anyone about my problems, worries, or fears. My mum and I barely talk and ours are not the confiding conversations that I think a mother and daughter should have. I'm scared I'll upset her, because once when we fought, we didn't talk to each other for almost two months, and I'm scared that will happen again. Who can I talk to that will listen and help me?"

PEER Responses

Write down your feelings

- You shouldn't (have to) feel the way you do – you need to learn how to get your feelings out, and learn how to express them and how to share them with someone who can help you. When you get irritated or angry, try to write down how you feel and what led to feeling that way, or just manically type out what you are thinking to get it out of your system to create a release.

- Take some time out, re-think/think over what's going on, and make a list of things you want to work on or wish to improve. Then, number this list, prioritizing items on what you want to fix. If it's an issue with friends, write out some names of trustworthy pals – focus on the good things that you have and the skills that you already have, rather than focusing on the negative.

Normalize your feelings/experience

- It sounds like this is not the 'ideal family', but that's okay! We do not choose our family, but we can choose our friends. Think about someone you can confide in and talk to.

- You shouldn't worry about your appearance – it doesn't change who you are.

- These are absolutely normal feelings to be having as a teenager – grades, boys, appearance – they are all part of high school; growing up is difficult.

- You're going to be okay!

Expand your social network

- Talk to people outside of your group: a schoolteacher you like and trust, or a school counselor.

- If you cannot confide in your friends (scared of embarrassment?), then maybe they aren't the group of people you should be dedicating your time to. Branch out, explore new friendships.

Communicate with your friends and your mother or other family members

- Tell your mates you don't like the teasing.

- Speak to your mom – let her know you need her.

- Maybe tell your mother how you feel – that might be the confiding talk you need to have with her.

- The way to rebuild your relationship with your mum is just by starting slow. Invite her to things you think she will be proud of you doing.

- What about your dad? Siblings? Consider these options.

PARENT Responses

Create avenues for communication

- Identify an adult you feel comfortable with and who you can ask if you can have a 'confidential' discussion with. Think about the people you know at school (teacher, counselor, supervisor), within your family (an aunt, uncle, cousin), or perhaps a parent of a friend.

- It is very important that you find someone to talk to. Try and share your concerns with someone to get the communication/ discussions started so that you can get the support that you need.

- Ask yourself: who do you see that has the character or integrity (personal principles) that you relate to or admire? Can you approach this individual and ask if you can have a 'confidential' discussion?

- You need some support to be able to learn how to put words to the feelings you are experiencing.

Consider contacting parent or other family members

- Tell your mom how you feel and find out why the two of you are not close enough to open up and discuss important 'growing up' related issues.

- It takes two people to make a relationship work. Think about what you can do to improve/work on/develop a better relationship with your mom. Let her know that you need her and want her as an important person in your life – as someone you can talk to, confide in, and go to for support.

Be mindful about well-being and how you address issues (especially nutrition)

- You need to identify and focus on positive aspects of your life. Ask yourself: what do you enjoy in life? How do you achieve enjoyment, both inside and outside of school? Find something you love about your life and try and find someone who can help and support you in identifying a goal in this pursuit. You might find some like-minded people as a result.

- Consider identifying a supportive adult you can talk to. Some of the things you describe are indicators of depression, something many teens experience. Tell yourself it is okay to have problems and difficulties as a teenager and, more importantly, that it is perfectly acceptable to ask those you trust for their help.

- There are 'tools' for coping with the difficulties that you are experiencing. Ask yourself: who is a person within your surroundings with whom you can discuss what you are going through? Try and approach this person and open up. Together you can work on finding the tools to help you!

Normalize experiences (validating) – this is normal in adolescence

- It is not unusual to have feelings like this during the teenage years – you are not alone.

- Being a teenager is difficult and sometimes overwhelming. You are not alone in feeling/experiencing this. You have to try and stop worrying about what others think and focus on what you feel and why. You clearly need to talk to someone. Maybe you would benefit from some support from a teacher, school counselor, or family member whom you can trust and to whom you can talk.

PROFESSIONAL Responses

Address your self-esteem issues

- It sounds like you have low self-esteem and possibly family/ relationship issues. Ask yourself what is contributing to this. Is there anything that makes you feel good about yourself?

- In what ways do you hurt people? Is it all people? What are your relationships like with the people in your class? Do you have any friends?

- You sound like you are isolated. You may want to consider finding ways to make yourself less isolated at school and enhance that outside of school (for example, consider going to social events to meet new people and build and develop new relationships).

- Do you hurt people because you don't have any other outlet for your distress? You may want to think about finding other outlets to relieve some of your disappointment and discomfort, such as playing an instrument, enrolling in drama classes, taking martial arts, volunteering at an animal shelter, or just going for a walk in the evenings.

Communicate

- Consider talking to other family members (siblings, cousins, grandparents) who might be able to give suggestions and/or support.

- Is your father in the picture? If so, consider going to him and getting some feedback about some of the things you described, including how to get along better with your mother. Chances are that if he was married to her and/or has known her for a long time, he may be able to give you advice that a stranger may not be able to.

- Is there anyone you would feel comfortable talking to, like a teacher, a school counselor, the school nurse, or a close friend in another country?

Promote your identity

- Focus on one or two things that you are good at and get in with a group of people who are also good at those things.

- Consider going to a school social event to meet other people.

Find balance

- Focus on the aspects that you can control, like ways to become organized so you can stay on top of your schoolwork; think about the things you are good at, think about the things you like; spend time thinking about the good things in your life – you need a bit more balance in your thoughts. When a person goes through a challenging period in life, it is easy to focus on the negative/bad/difficult things and completely forget about all of the good/positive/fun things. Maybe make a list to 'see' how you feel about your life. Include the positive and the negative/challenging in order to be honest with yourself, and analyze things from a more balanced perspective.

- Consider talking to your teachers about ways that you can balance your load and effectively plan for projects, tests, and so on. Let them know that you need some support.

Validate your feelings

- Know that you are not alone! What are the primary problems and who can help with those? Answer the question: "What is the worst thing that can happen?"

- Recognize that there are others who may share similar difficulties and concerns.

Find a safe environment

- Making the decision to talk to someone takes courage. It also takes a trusting and confidential environment that is comfortable for you. If you don't feel that you have access to this, reach out to someone you may have trusted in the past, like a friend or family member in a different country.

Seek help from school or an advocate

- Seek help from a senior mentor or school counselor who could help you work through your concerns and who could also possibly be an advocate for you as you consider talking to your mother about your relationship with her.

- Sometimes talking to a school counselor seems weird or embarrassing for various reasons, including the fact that you don't want anyone else to know that you are doing so. Consider dropping into the counselor's office during lunchtime when most other people are too busy eating to take notice. Or consider staying after school to chat with a teacher that you trust.

- Consider suggesting to your school (through a pastoral care coordinator, homeroom teacher, or head of year/grade) that they have small group lessons in school (i.e. during homeroom or pastoral care lessons) that focus on social issues and perceptions.

- Consider talking to the school nurse, your family doctor, or a nutritionist about appropriate ways to lose weight, as well as about ways to help you fall asleep and then sleep well.

- Work with your advisor, counselor, or mentor on setting academic goals, and follow up with the person to give updates on your progress.

Expat Teens say...

"Are you stressed...? Yeah, well, we all are. You're not alone."

PERSONAL REFLECTIONS

'Little fish in a big pond'

"I wasn't born into a rich family, but I get the impression that most of the international students I go to school with were. I came to the school that I'm currently attending from a country far away just to study. Before I came, I thought, I don't need to compare myself to my peers about anything except my grades. *I thought that as long as I was friendly and well-balanced, I would win the respect of my peers. But I was wrong.*

Language is a big problem. I'm not a native English speaker, and I always fall behind in my English class. All of the other students around me actively participate; however, I find myself keeping quiet all the time. I sometimes think I know how to express myself, but I'm afraid of giving the wrong answer.

I used to be unique in my old school because of my many talents – I am musically talented, I have competed very well in different sports, and I have always achieved high grades, which made me stand out (positively) from my peers. Here (in this international school) it is very different. What I can do, my new peers can do even better. Everything that used to make me proud and unique just seems to be common here. I feel somewhat pressured by my peers in this environment because I feel like I'm just not good enough. Because of that, I feel like I am falling behind. I have nothing that sets me apart now. I'm having a really hard time adjusting to and identifying my role in this environment."

PEER Responses

Don't worry about putting yourself forward

- It takes time to adjust to new system of education. Allow yourself the time to adjust, settle in, and focus on identifying and meeting your own needs.

- Materialism and monetary values are only peripheral; focus on who you are, what you need, what you like, and your personal strengths.

- Don't be afraid to speak just because you think it might be wrong. If you don't think you're as good as others around you, think about and remind yourself what you are good at. Pursue what you are good at and what you enjoy; eventually people will recognize you as a unique individual because of it. Try and socialize with others who have the same interests like music and sports.

- Don't worry and over-think this situation. You're right – you don't have to compare yourself to others! Everyone is different! Be proud of your differences, as they make you special!

Have confidence

- Don't feel pressured. The most important thing is to know that you are doing the best that you can do. Feel proud of yourself and acknowledge all the things that you have achieved, as that's all that really matters! Compare yourself to yourself and nobody else, as that is a sign of self-confidence!

- Why be afraid? There is no need to be afraid of being wrong. Mistakes are the 'stepping stones' to achieving success.

- Remind yourself that you are not alone. Others have gone, and are going, though similar experiences. There is always something that sets us apart as individuals and makes us different.

- Remind yourself that, regardless of the others around you, you are talented and successful.

- Know that you are in an established school and, therefore, competition will be tough! Rise to the new challenges that you are presented with, and see them as positive and motivating to improve your own personal best. Start developing the mindset 'if they can do it, so can I!' Believe in yourself.

- Understand that there are always people better and worse than you at various activities, around the world.

- As long as you believe in yourself and do the best you can do, that's all that matters.

Find help – someone to talk to for social and emotional support

- Talk to someone. What you are thinking and believing is one point of view, and you need to hear feedback about what you feel and what you are going through from a different perspective.

- You need to talk to someone who can help you find something you enjoy rather than trying to, or feeling like you have to, be perfect in areas you were previously successful in. Confiding in someone who can help will prevent you from spiraling into a depression, which is a realistic risk you run if you do not seek support.

Find help for language

- Language is a barrier, which is currently preventing you from exposing and sharing your talents in an international school. Ask for some language support, and keep practicing your English.

- Talk to your teachers and ask for advice or share how you feel. They are there to help you and you are not the first teenager in an international school environment with a language 'barrier'.

Make connections with others

- Try to find new activities in which you can develop new skills through which you can thrive and feel good about yourself again.

- Remember: we are all unique! You are from a country far away, but remind yourself of all the things you can offer, contribute, and share with those in your new environment as a result of your differences.

- While it may appear that your peers have a stronger skill set than you, don't put yourself down! If you truly enjoy your hobbies, then you will continue to excel. Appreciate the people around you – learn from them, and turn your negative mindset into a positive opportunity and gain from it. You are unique – embrace this!

- Open up, walk in the shoes of others for a while, and try to see things from their perspective. What you are going through is part of a greater experience, one that benefits you for life. Things may not be the same as what you knew, but you have been given an opportunity to learn, so maximize it. Change is good – embrace it!

PARENT Responses

Put financial assumptions in perspective

- There are many students and families at international schools who are perceived as being rich. The reality is that there is a mix of families from very different socioeconomic backgrounds and statuses. Those who are not rich attend the same international schools as those who are. This is not much different from many national schools in monocultural environments where the rich attend schools alongside the non-rich.

- Fellow expatriates, teachers, and students are wrong to assume every expat is wealthy. Many people perceive expats as wealthy as they have to pay high fees for international schools, often live in housing that is higher than what they would pay for the equivalent 'standard' of housing in their own country, and travel more than their local counterparts. There are huge discrepancies in financial status in expat communities, just as there are in local communities. Not every expat is wealthy.

- Money isn't everything. Try and get to know the people around you. Get past what you perceive as their family financial status. There is so much more to these individuals to discover and learn about than how much money their families are worth.

- Why are you judging those around you by their financial status? You do not have to compare yourself to them nor compare them to each other based on money. Try and look beyond this.

Try not to make comparisons

- International schools often have a melting pot of nationalities amongst the student, teacher, and parent bodies. Every individual has different strengths and weaknesses. One student may be brilliant in math, while you, yourself, excel with your many talents.

- Take advantage of the opportunities you are presented with in your new environment. Maximize your exposure to the facilities you are exposed to, spend more time with teachers and coaches, continue learning and further developing your own abilities in your new environment.

- Rather than looking at the others as better than you and putting yourself down as a result, why don't you set new targets for yourself? Take advantage of the expertise around you and continue to learn and enjoy what you are already good at.

Build your language confidence

- Feeling insecure or inadequate with a language can be frustrating. Surely your international school is familiar with this as a challenge? Find out where the ESOL (English as a second or other language) department is and ask for further support.

- Inquire about peer tutoring at your school. The best way to improve any language is to actively use it. If you feel shy or insecure using your English language skills in the classroom, then spend more time using and practicing them outside of the classroom. Working with peer tutors will give you an advantage of being able to develop new relationships with students in your new school.

- Find out from the school admissions department if there are other students of the same nationality and language background. Find these students and learn from them how they dealt with and overcame the language barrier.

- Try and change your mindset to be more solutions-focused. Often students forget that teachers are there to work with you, to support and help you with all academic and most social issues. Let them know that you are struggling, and ask for guidance in finding the support that you need.

Allow yourself to feel special

- You are unique and you are special. Think about all of the different things that you are good at: sports, music, and academics. Many students are content with having strengths in one area, but you seem to have strengths in many. Recognize that and feel proud!

- You have developed strengths in a variety of areas, so use this as an advantage for developing your social network and your language development and for further developing the things you are already good at. Find an entry point at your school into the music and sports department. Work on building positive relationships with other students who share your interest in sport and music, and at the same time, work on improving your already developed skills and abilities. Who says you cannot improve on what you are already good at? Your advantage is that you already have more than the basic abilities on which to continue building.

PROFESSIONAL Responses

Find language support

- Talk with your language teacher about ways to be more confident in class. If getting help at school is too intimidating, consider taking language classes in the community.

- Let your language teacher know your concerns about saying the wrong thing and ask him/her how to overcome that – use the teacher as an ally in class (i.e. a source of encouragement and support).

- Find opportunities to practice English with trusted peers and maybe even a mentor. Then, go with them into the community so that you can practice your English with someone else who can support you.

- Consider talking to the school counselor as he or she may be able to give you some good advice on how to cope.

Maintain support from home country

- Keep in touch with your friends from your home country, as they should be able to provide you with the support that you need.

- Find out if there are other students from your former school who may have ventured out of the country to go to school like you did. Get support from them and find out how they managed the experience.

- Maintain contact with your family for support.

Seek support from other scholars

- Ask your guidance counselor, the person in charge of scholarship students, or the person in charge of transfer students about other students (either from your home country or from other countries where English is not a primary language) with whom you could meet and discuss your common experiences.

- Keep being friendly and well balanced, because that *is* a way to make friends! If others are not receptive to your attempts to make friends, then maybe you need to look at meeting people in other groups at school or in locations outside of school. Having supportive friends can make a huge difference for you.

- Consider meeting up with some of the students for dinner and try to get to know them a little more before you make judgments. They may be trying just as hard as you and could also be missing their hometown.

Adjust your mindset

- Not all expats are rich! A great deal of them come from their countries as 'ordinary students'. Sometimes, parents have more disposable income and, therefore, it seems like their children have all of the latest gizmos, but most are just 'ordinary'.

- You used to stand out in your former school, which made you a 'big fish in a small pond'. Now, you are 'just like everyone else', which makes you a 'small fish in a big pond'. Start to see this as a good thing – that you are in a place where *everyone* strives for excellence! Use it as a challenge to improve yourself.

- Try not to compare yourself to others – focus on comparing your current accomplishments to your previous accomplishments (from before you moved), and find the positives within your experience.

- You seem to be low on confidence. Know what you can do and do it well!

- Set personal and academic goals for yourself and focus on those instead of on what everyone else is doing.

Get involved

- Find a group in the community that is culture-specific to your home country. This could include being part of a culture-specific club (for example, the Dutch Club, the German Club, the Japanese Society), or part of an embassy group (for example, the Chinese Embassy, the French Embassy). Find out about activities that they have and consider attending these so that you can be around others who have the same culture and language as you do.

- Engage in something that makes you happy (for example, yoga, tap classes or singing)! It is important to do activities like this, as it will help keep your self-esteem intact, and some activities can be done without having to rely on speaking the local language.

Expat Teens say...

"Being an Expat Teen means not knowing the meaning of 'exotic'."

PERSONAL REFLECTIONS

'Don't judge a book by its cover'

"As an Expat Teen, I feel challenged by society today. The inappropriate behaviour and attitudes of my peers are irritating and disturbing. They won't leave me alone – they judge me based on the way I look, the way I behave, and the way I speak. From my point of view, they are judging me by what they see and hear without trying to get to know me. For example, at school, when I sit at a table with 'friends', some of the people around us get up and leave or sit as far away from us as they can. Some of these same people pick on me – they touch and disturb my possessions and won't stop or leave me alone until I get really upset and strike out physically. I feel pressured and bullied and do not know what to do."

PEER Responses

Get others on your team, befriend those who the bullies look up to

- These individuals may be behaving like this because they get a 'thrill' out of the reaction they can provoke from you. Do not stoop to their level – rise above them, because you are better than that!

- You sound like an intellectual thinker. Rise above these peers with your words! Outsmart them and make them realize how immature and ridiculous they are being. Do not give them the thrill by reacting according to how they want/predict/provoke you to react.

- Ignore them – eventually they will get bored and stop.

- Confront these peers and their immature behavior and/or contact the school authorities. There will be other peers in your school community who will admire and respect you for taking action and showing strong leadership qualities.

Be strong and be yourself – resilience and coping

- Be yourself and be patient with those who are creating stress in your life.

- Take a step back and think about who your real friends are – those you feel close to, trust and can confide in. Work on further developing these more important relationships, because these people you refer to are not 'true friends'.

Tell teachers and others about what is going on

- Bullying is a serious and destructive offense. This is something that could potentially spiral out of control, and you cannot ignore it. Take action by reporting the behavior. Talk to someone at school who you can trust and who will give you advice and support about how to best deal with the situation; someone who will assist you in a professional manner that ensures that it does not become worse for you as a result.

- This may be a trend of behavior in the school, so put a stop to it by getting teachers and counselors involved. You are already a victim, but there may be others, so take the lead and help put a stop to this for everyone.

Rise above the conflict

- Involve yourself in extracurricular activities like sports. Get involved and keep busy doing things you like with people who share the same interests.

- You have to be aware of the fact that the qualities that define you will often differ from the qualities that define your peers. Embrace your differences as they make you special.

- High school can be a very scary place, and you need to be strong to get through it. Do not let those who are bullying you or treating you badly get the upper hand.

Take on other roles, especially roles of leadership

- Find a way to develop roles of leadership. Put yourself in a better position where people can look up to you and listen to what you have to say. Join the student council, the peer support group, the debate club, or other clubs/teams that enable you to have a 'voice' that will be heard.

Talk to family or other important people in your life

- Discuss this with your parents and counselors.

- You do not have to deal with this alone. Talk to your parents, your real friends, and to counselors at school. There are people around you who can and will help.

PARENT Responses

Give yourself permission to remove yourself from situations

- This is not a uniquely Expat Teen experience. In fact, being an expat can mean eventual relief as a result of a new assignment and move. But it can also mean being confronted by similar situations again and again. The one good thing is that the Expat Teen writing this submission sees this as the other teens' problem and isn't internalizing by asking 'What's wrong with me?' This Expat Teen has a strong sense of self that needs to be celebrated and fostered. Schools should be on top of every bullying situation, because it is a serious issue.

Remember that you are in control, you have choices

- You have the freedom to choose your friends!

- Sometimes we need to be reminded that we have choices. You do not have to accept intolerable behavior of others, so think about your choices and make them.

- Acknowledge that this is a difficulty and not an easy situation to deal with. Give yourself permission to draw perimeters around the world you envision for yourself. Decide for yourself who you want to let in to that world. Give yourself permission to remove yourself from situations that make you unhappy.

- Remember, this will pass! Stay firm and strong in your beliefs. Think about who you are and who you want to be. It's painful to be strong and it hurts to be rejected. BUT think about who is doing this to you – are they worth it? You DO have choices.

- Don't take behavior that crosses your boundaries. Physically stand up and say, "You can't talk to me that way!" Remove yourself from bad situations. You are NOT alone! As much as it sometimes looks and feels that way, and gives the impression that everyone else 'fits' in, you would be surprised to learn about everyone else who carries their own pain or troubles.

It's not about you, it's about them

- Speak frankly to those who bully you and in simple language. Say, for example, "I don't understand why you do this to me – it really hurts my feelings."

Surround yourself with like-minded people

- Find activities, hobbies, sports – things you can involve yourself in to be surrounded by like-minded individuals. Be around and spend time with people you like and who like doing the same things as you. Get involved and spend your time positively.

- Real friends will not judge you for the way you dress. They'll know and appreciate you for who you really are. You do not have to change who you are to accommodate others. There are plenty of people out there, so maybe you're not choosing the right ones to surround yourself with. Take time to reflect upon who you surround yourself with and why, then think about what type of people you want to be with and why. Find a way to meet those people.

Get help, support

- Confide in a teacher, counselor, or mentor at school about what is going on. Get the support they are responsible for giving you.

- Find resources to empower yourself – talk to family and parents and explain your issues. Your home is a 'safe haven' – it is a place you can always come to, to be yourself and to get support. Allow yourself to step out of the trouble zone for a bit to reboot in the safe zone. Your family is always your family, whereas friends in an expat environment often come and go.

PROFESSIONAL Responses

Be open-minded, consider support from other peers, school or the internet

- You say, "… they are judging me by what they see and hear without trying to get to know me." Have you tried to get to know them or are you perhaps also judging them without knowing them? Forming good relationships is a two-way street. Ask your peers about their lives – how they grew up, where they have lived, what their favorite country was, what kind of music they like, what bothers them, what they worry about. Learn to listen. Once you have asked questions about their lives, they are more likely to want to get to know you better. You may find that you have more in common with each other than either of you think.

- You may also want to try making a new group of friends. Get involved with clubs, sports, and activities you enjoy, where you can meet people with common interests.

- If you are still feeling bullied, it is important to let the school administration know about it. There are many things the school can do to prevent bullying and support victims of bullying.

- **Here is some information about bullying from the National Crime Prevention Council (www.ncpc.org/newsroom/current-campaign/bully-prevention):** "Most bullying happens when adults aren't around, such as in between classes, at lunch or recess, after school, and online. Still, bullying rarely takes place without an audience – kids are around to see bullying 85 percent of the time. But even though they see it, kids usually don't try to stop bullying, and may even be unknowingly encouraging it.

- Most of the time that kids witness bullying, they stand by passively. This causes bullying to last longer because it reinforces the bullies' power and status: two reasons why people bully. Most kids don't want to watch bullying, and don't want it to happen at all. But many kids don't know how to stop it and worry that by stepping in they might become the next victim. These worries, and witnessing verbal and physical abuse, take a toll on bystanders.

- There are effective and safe ways for kids to step in and help others being bullied. Some work better in certain situations than others. Remember that kids should only step in when they feel safe.

- **Walk away.** This shows bullies that their behavior is not funny or okay.

- **Speak up.** Tell bullies that what they are doing is wrong. By saying, "That's not funny, let's get out of here" or something similar, kids can stand up for each other. This may also give other bystanders the confidence to speak up or walk away.

- **Be a friend.** Sometimes kids get picked on because they don't have any friends or anyone to stand up for them. When kids befriend someone being bullied, bullies are less likely to pick on them. Friendship can also give children the support and the confidence to stand up for themselves.

- **Ask others to help.** When more kids stand up to bullies, the bullies will be more likely to realize their actions are not okay.

- **Get an adult.** Sometime kids who are bullied are scared to ask an adult for help because they think it will make the bullying worse. Kids can help by telling an adult what is happening, or going to speak to an adult with kids being bullied."

Expat Teens say...

"Being an Expat Teen means all experiences, cultures, countries and languages have affected your life in some way."

PERSONAL REFLECTIONS

"Growing up as an Expat Teen seems to be about 'a lot more'. For example, I feel like Expat Teens have a lot more pressure on them from parents to perform well at school. I think attending private international schools means being confronted by a lot more school work, academic demands, activities, and expectations. I feel like I, personally, have a lot of support from my family here, which makes things easier. However, I am most worried about moving back to my home country (which we will do eventually). There, I will be seen by my peers as being different because I have lived abroad. This is in addition to being 'the new kid' and not fitting in."

PEER Responses

Be proud of yourself

- Embrace being different – it makes you special.

- Embrace the diversity of your experiences; recognize your experiences as positive, and think of this as a way to make you unique; this is an advantage for you. When returning to your home country, you will have the ability to teach them about the rest of the world and your personal experiences through international exposure. Think about it – it is cool to be different.

- Do the best you can and embrace your life experiences, as they contribute to forming who you are.

Share your experiences with the local community

- When you eventually move back to your home country, turn your experiences into something positive. Being the new kid who has lived in many different countries, and has been a part of and seen lots of different things around the world, can make you the 'cool/interesting' new kid. Not everyone has international exposure; it does make you special in a positive way.

- Introduce and share your life experiences with others when you return home. Be open to the differences and embrace them, learn from them, share them.

Keep in touch with expat friends

- Access to the internet makes staying in touch easy. Take advantage of what you have access to and share your new life with your old friends.

Recognize the benefits of an international school education; grow from and look at education as a blueprint for life

- Try and think about how lucky you are and enjoy your opportunities as a result of your expat life. Everything you experience will better prepare you for the future. 'What doesn't kill you makes you stronger.'

- International schools often have broader choices related to sports, activities, and courses, as a result of having to cater to so many different nationalities and expectations. This is an advantage, so use it and maximize these opportunities. Enjoy the challenges of more, harder, challenging; this is all part of being an Expat Teen and being exposed to a lot of change. Maximize the positive advantages – see them for what they are and benefit from them.

- Be proud to be an international student!

PARENT Responses

Make 'being different' a positive experience

- Think about all the wonderful qualities you have acquired as a result of your international experience. You have clearly grown in being more culturally aware and sensitive to differences. Being different can be extremely positive as you have something to add, something to share to a new peer group.

- Moving from an international environment to a monocultural environment will inevitably make you more aware of how much you have changed, grown, and experienced as a result of having lived abroad. These changes will make you stronger and more mature in your ability to recognize and adapt to the changes you will be confronted with when moving to a more local, monocultural environment.

- Take your 'tool box' with you when you move. You have clearly managed to adapt to an international environment where you were confronted by 'more'. Think about the skills you have developed to enable you to do this. Believe in yourself; adapting to being the 'new kid' in a new environment is something you can do well.

- The peers in your new environment may not have had the experience of having lived abroad, but they may be able to relate to different countries, languages, and cultures as a result of having traveled.

Make the most of 'more'

- Adapting to a busy, cultural melting pot in an international school can be a high-pressure situation. Many international school students do all of their activities at school, for example – competitive sports, playing an instrument, participating in the school band, drama clubs, plays, arts programme, and so on. In many expat communities, it is difficult, if not impossible, to integrate into the local communities of the host country as a result of the cultural, language, and (sometimes) religious barrier. This inevitably makes the international school the community for the expats. Doing everything in one location does make for a busy place, giving the impression of 'more'.

- Growing up in an international school exposes you to students and teachers from all over the world. Your school will likely have a structured curriculum, but the expectations of teachers will vary as a result of their professional and personal backgrounds. Students' attitudes, commitments, and efforts will also vary depending on their cultural backgrounds and experiences, which will impact their personal expectations.

- Whether or not an international school accepts local students can also impact the dynamics and attitudes towards academic success. Some cultures, for example, tend to be more academically competitive than others, creating the impression of having to try harder and work more to live up to the same standards for those students from less competitive cultural backgrounds.

Celebrate being 'different'

- As a parent of Expat Teens, I would encourage my kids to have the confidence to have fun being different rather than be scared of it. When my own Expat Kids go to sports camps in our home country (not the country we currently live in) they are given so much positive attention and the other kids are so interested in where they are from – never has it been a negative experience. So, perhaps when moving back, you would be seen as interesting rather than odd.

- Another parent of an Expat Teen recently shared the experience of her Expat Teen, who went off to study in the family's home country and was very popular from the start because of having lived abroad. It was a positive experience and easy to settle in with local peers. Try to see your differences as an advantage rather than disadvantage.

- We are all a bit different from living this life, but it makes us interesting people with such a broad base of what 'normal' is. We could fit in anywhere and roll with the changes easily.

- Being a bit bored would be more of a worry than people thinking one is boring – in that respect, keeping in touch with friends from your Expat Life would be important. I think being an Expat Kid is to be an expert on adapting, and that 'fitting in' wouldn't be the issue. Quickly finding kids who do a similar sport or hobby would be key to settling in well and being accepted.

PROFESSIONAL Responses

Stay connected and get involved

- If you keep in touch by visiting home and keeping in contact with your friends, this will go a long way towards easing your transition.

- Get involved in a club or sport or other activity that will help you settle in, as this will help you remember what it was like to be part of your home environment.

Use your experiences to your advantage

- You have been abroad, so everyone will find you very interesting, initially. They will be fascinated by the language(s) you speak, where you have traveled to, and the school environments that you have been exposed to.

- You may find that you are ahead of the game, academically, which can be a positive thing!

- You may have developed greater empathy for students at your home school, especially if they come from different racial and religious backgrounds. In addition, they may have religious practices or celebrations that you have experienced, so you may have the opportunity to talk to them about those experiences – in their native language!

What you are feeling is normal!

- There is a growing trend in many countries worldwide of more and more pressure being exerted on high school students to achieve, be well rounded, and perform well academically in order to get into the 'right' college or university. International school students competing for these same spots are also feeling the pressure to develop the profile that will give them an edge in the application process. The good news is that international school students often come out ahead of their domestic peers with a solid work ethic, good study habits, and excellent educational foundations that allow them to confront the challenges of college/university with confidence.

- Your concern of not fitting in when you return to your home country is a common theme amongst Third Culture Kids. As you have said, your international experiences will undoubtedly make you feel different from most of the people you will be surrounded by. You do not share common experiences of growing up with them. It is important to remember that although you may feel like you don't fit in, it doesn't mean there is anything wrong with you. *The Global Nomad's Guide to University Transition*, by Tina L. Quick, is a wonderful new resource that addresses all the important issues Third Culture Kids face when they return home, whether it is for college/university or high school.

Expat Teens say...

"Being an Expat Teen means never hearing your name being pronounced the right way."

PERSONAL REFLECTIONS

CHAPTER FOUR:
Sex, drugs and alcohol

> ## 'Freedom can be hazardous to your health: everything in moderation'
>
> *"In my opinion, as an Expat Teen, we have more freedom than teens growing up in their home countries, as our parents think we are more mature. I can honestly say that most Expat Teens take advantage of that freedom. For example, I have a fake ID, I go clubbing at least once a week, I get drunk at least once a week, and I have sex on a regular basis. This is what I enjoy and I don't want it to stop anytime soon. And I do know for a fact that many of my peers are engaging in the same behaviours."*

PEER Responses:

Think about the laws of the country

- Is your city a safe place to do this under age?

- What are the punishments for doing these things under age?

- Though what you say may be true, take a step back and look at the situation: regardless of how "mature" your parents think you are, there is a law which one is expected to obey.

- Just because you are an expat does not make you an exception (to the rules of the country).

- Be careful with this freedom – you may get into trouble and, especially in a foreign country, this behavior could affect your parents.

Don't assume that all Expat Teens are doing the same thing

- Not everyone is like this. People that grow up in their home country also do these things.

- It's a false statement that "most Expat Teens" engage in the same behaviors.

Don't abuse your parents' trust

- I wouldn't say it is because your parents think you are more mature – it is most likely because they are looser with you because they think the country you are in is safer.

- Be careful with the freedoms.

- Don't abuse/take advantage of your parents' trust. Don't give them a reason not to trust you.

- Take advantage of the liberties you have and show your parents that you are responsible.

Be honest with your parents

- Slowly let your parents know what you are doing.

- Being honest with your parents can often assure your liberty, as well as build trust and provide support and communication as needed.

- Ask your parents what they did during their teenage years – were they involved in similar activities?

- Keep your parents on your side.

- Make sure your parents are okay with it. If you disobey them, your whole life could be shut down.

Don't put yourself in a situation (just) because you think others are doing the same thing

- Keep it up IF you enjoy it – don't feel pressured to do it and don't care what people think if it's what *you* want. However, be careful, because things like fake IDs can have negative consequences.

- You may enjoy it now, but you will probably stop liking it later on in life and it will get too monotonous.

- Don't kid yourself – don't put yourself in these situations just because you are pretty sure that your friends are doing it.

- Don't engage in more activities than you can handle.

Think about safety and natural consequences

- Wear a condom.

- Don't do drugs.

- Do not push the limits – be cautious.

- Make sure it doesn't go too far. For example, it sounds like pregnancy could be an issue (or risk) for you and it would pretty much shut down your whole life.

- Be safe and honest.

Don't pressure others into what you are doing/ consider your reputation

- REMEMBER: you influence other people – friends, peers, family. So be considerate of your influences and power, because this can create a negative reputation and can impact your future.

- If other people aren't comfortable with this DO NOT be that kid that pressures them into it!

- First impressions as a new student DO matter!

- It's hard to shake off this reputation once it has been established.

Remember the impact on your future

- These behaviors could jeopardize your academics/ schooling – don't let them become a distraction.

- There is always the possibility that you could become addicted (to the substances; to this type of lifestyle).

- Understand your parents' values and consider them yourself, especially as you think about your future.

- Think about the problems that may spark from this – low grades, poor relationships with parents/others, damaging your brain, getting addicted, running yourself into a hole.

- Remember that, while this may appear to be 'the good life', academics, sports, and friends are more important. These behaviors physically and mentally affect you in the long term.

- I understand it may be hard to admit to change, but talk to your friends honestly about this and prioritize. You have to remember that there will always be consequences to your actions, so don't abuse them.

Live so that you have no regrets

- Keep your social life and work life separate. Don't let partying take a toll on your grades – it will come back to bite you.

- As much as you enjoy the situation and the liberty presented, you are a CHILD: Enjoy it! You don't want to look back at this point in your life and have regrets at becoming too mature too fast. These years, you should still be learning, and not in terms of alcohol tolerance.

- Respect your childhood – you only get one!

Understand why your parents have rules

- Think about why your parents apply rules – it is not purposely to harm you but to help you.

- Be aware of the effect that this behavior has on your siblings or close friends – you may be hurting people and you may not be aware of it.

Seek other interests/enjoy your surroundings

- Keep your old friends, but maybe spend time with a new group.

- If this (your current activities) is all you've known, then you might want to try something new (even though you like your current activities).

- Observe the surroundings you are in (and find other things to do that you may like or that may be more interesting/fulfilling).

PARENT Responses

You need your own moral compass/consider your reputation/others' perceptions of you

- Family principles and morals should be consistent both when you are an expat teen and when you are not.

- Each environment (new country/city) will have a set of 'rules', but you as teens – Expat Teens – need to have innate values no matter where in the world you live.

- Be responsible and make decisions you feel good about, decisions that do not undermine your principles.

- Your reputation follows you and, to outsiders, defines you. Live your life with a positive moral compass that you can live by.

- Teens and parents of teens are very quick to profile and label others. Take the time to think about how your current behaviors may impact the impression others have of you. How does that honestly make you feel?

Take responsibility

- You, and only you, are responsible for yourself. You are engaging in some very risky behaviors. Because you feel you have the 'freedom' to act this way does not mean that you should or that your parents condone it. Take a moment to ask yourself these questions:

  o 1. Am I prepared to deal with the repercussions of my sexual behavior (pregnancy, abortion, sexually transmitted diseases)?

  o 2. Do my friends engage in the same behaviors? Do I seek the limelight? Do I need to reassess?

- Be aware that, at a young age, the behaviors that you engage in often define 'who you are', and are not restricted to 'what you do'. There is a huge difference. Think about who you are and who you want to be – there is still time to change.

- To a certain degree, you may be right in expressing that you have more freedoms. Many Expat Parents do travel extensively, leaving 'responsible' teens behind under the supervision of a household helper or a friend. However, having more freedom is a huge responsibility. You may be unsupervised, therefore having more freedom, but are you safe?

- Ask yourself: would you want a child of your own engaging in the same behaviors as you are at your age? Why or why not? And why wouldn't you apply the guidelines to yourself? You are important, so take care of yourself in the same manner that you would take care of someone you were responsible for.

Be mindful of safety and education

- Make sure that you are taking the necessary precautions to ensure your safety! If you are not sure what these are, then you should make an appointment with a school counsellor and ask. Inform and educate yourself!

- If you feel you are mature enough to be engaging in these behaviours, then be mature enough to engage in them without risk.

- During adolescence and puberty, one tends to explore and experiment. Remind yourself that it is NOT okay to do everything. Be informed, make safe decisions and protect yourself.

- Expat Teen experiences do, indeed, give you unique opportunities and challenges. Ensure that you communicate respect for the environment in which you live (i.e. your host country).

- You are engaging in behaviors that have consequences that are difficult to deal with for a teenager, regardless of where in the world you live. For example, pregnancy is a consequence of engaging in unprotected sex. It can have huge impacts on the entire family if this occurs in a 'host country', pending the laws related to the legal age of sexual consent, the attitudes and openness towards adoption/abortion/having choices, and so on.

Communicate

- Have you confided in anyone about the behaviors you are engaging in? You may want to consider talking to someone to make sure that you are fully aware of the impact that your behaviors could have on your health and, potentially, your future.

Involve your parents

- Discuss your behaviors with your parents. They should know what you are doing and, therefore, take on the responsibility of ensuring that you are acting in a safe and self- respecting manner.

Know the values of the surrounding culture

- You are making a big assumption in saying that all Expat Teens have more freedoms and access. Be honest with yourself – this is not the case.

Consider other social alternatives

- Ask yourself what your interests and passions are – how can you pursue these to ensure that you invest the time and maximize opportunities to prepare for your future? You are going through an enormous period of change – take the time to think and reflect, identify what your meaningful priorities are and pursue them. Take the time to ensure that you make choices and engage in activities about which you feel good and proud.

If you do not do these things it's okay

- It sounds like you could benefit from sharing your point of view – and behaviors – with a counselor. Sometimes we think we are mature enough and have the life experience to make decisions we will always feel good about. Ask yourself if this is the case, and take the time to discuss with a professional why you engage in these behaviors and how you feel you benefit from them.

PROFESSIONAL Responses

Be aware of issues related to safety and health

- Make sure you understand the consequences of your behavior and be safe if you choose to engage in these behaviors.

- How do you look after yourself when you are out, particularly if you are using substances? Do you go out with other people so that there is at least one person who can be responsible for getting you home safely?

- Are you ever the one looking after your friends when you go out, or do they always have to look after you? Have you ever ended up in a situation that you could not get out of? When you have these feelings of helplessness, what do you do about them? Do they alter the choices you make for the next outing?

- You seem to be significantly minimizing the harm and risk that is involved. Do you even know the dangers involved with what you are doing?

Know your boundaries and respect the authority

- If people at your school know about what you do on a regular basis, they should be talking with your parents directly. Many schools have a policy about these kinds of behaviors, even when you are not on school grounds.

- The responsibility may be on the school to provide parent information evenings, coffee mornings, PTA meetings, and so on to address these issues within the school community. Similar discussions should be had with students during curriculum or advisory meetings and could be focused on open conversation and/or involve a talk from the police or other law enforcement outlining the legal consequences of these behaviors.

- What are the consequences if you get caught? Who would be affected if you got caught?

- The school should be very clear about what they expect from you and your peers, both on campus, as well as off campus. They should also be very clear about what the consequences are for breaking those rules. If you are fully informed and choose to engage in those activities anyway, then you will be actively breaking those rules, which means that you are okay with the consequences.

- If you decide to stop engaging in these activities, it will be important for you and your parents to identify the boundaries and expectations that they have for you, and for you to work hard to maintain those boundaries and expectations, because this is practice for life as an adult.

Consider parental involvement

- Do you have an open conversation with your parents about your actions and the choices you are making? How involved are they?

- Your parents should have a 'worst case scenario' discussion with you, which would allow all of you to open up about the consequences of your behavior, and a reality check that your behavior has consequences for everyone in the family.

- Sometimes we use fake behaviors when we may be hurting due to being or feeling neglected. Is this the case for you? If so, could you find some way of expressing those feelings of hurt more appropriately? How would your parents respond to an appropriate request for their attention?

- It is important for your parents to be more involved in knowing where you are and what you are doing. Your current decisions will impact your future, and your parents are in a good position to be able to reinforce that with you on a regular basis.

Consider issues related to trust

- Are you sure your parents would trust you if they knew exactly what you were doing and how often you were doing it?

- It seems as though you are misusing your freedoms. Have you ever wondered why you are doing this? Aside from it being fun, what else do you get from engaging in these behaviors? Is it worth the risk (to your body, your family, your reputation)?

Be realistic

- How do you know for sure that everyone engages in the activities that you describe? If you really think about it, how many of your friends actually do these things versus how many *say* they are doing them? Can you really answer that question? Do you really know?

- Do you feel like you have ever made any mistakes while you've been out doing these things? If so, did you learn from them?

- Past behavior is the best predictor of future behavior. If you reflect on that and then think about what you just described, is this how you want your current friends to remember you? Is this how you want your future friends and family (including a romantic partner) to know you? Are these activities 'child's play', or are they demons that will follow you forever? How do you know? Do you care? Rest assured that at least some your current and future family and friends do/will...

Have self-control (minimize risk, keep discussion open)

- How would your life change if you changed these behaviors?

- Is there anything else (appropriate activities) that you enjoy? Could you get others involved in those things along with you so that none of you feel like you have to follow the people who engage in the activities you described?

Be educated about all of this (both parent and child)

- There is a connection between feelings and behavior. What is going on inside of you that is making you choose to engage in these activities? Is it *purely* that you want to have a good time and enjoy these activities, or is there something else (Emptiness? A desire for boundaries?) that is prompting this behavior?

- The school should consider having parent information sessions to focus on maturity (or lack thereof), statistics related to these types of behaviors, boundaries (how to set them and maintain them), and ways to encourage open-minded discussions.

Know the peer expectations (including, what to say to peers if you decide to give up that lifestyle)

- Do your peers really expect you to engage in these activities? If so, what does that say about your own self-confidence or self-esteem? If you are struggling with your own sense of self, is there anyone you can talk to about that so that you don't continue to engage in self-destructive activities?

- If you decide to stop engaging in these behaviors, it would be helpful for you to seek out someone (peer, adult, parent) to talk to about it and to help you start participating in other activities that are more appropriate.

Expat Teens say...

"Being an Expat Teen means that you can swear in at least four different languages."

PERSONAL REFLECTIONS

CHAPTER FIVE:
Family relationships

> ## *'Lost in translation'*
>
> *"My parents are divorced, so I can't talk to my dad, because I haven't seen him in about five months and I don't think he cares about me. My little sister doesn't care and my older sisters don't live with us, and my other family members live in my home country, and/or are too busy to care about my problems. My mum is always busy. She tries her best, but I do not feel I can burden her with my problems. My mum is struggling with the divorce and so am I. I don't feel like I have anyone I can I talk to when I have a bad day or feel upset."*

PEER Responses

Talk to your siblings

- Talk to your older sisters. They felt it too, so make the effort to get in contact (via Skype). Since they used to live at home with the same parents as you, they could probably give some good advice. Surely they care – maybe they just don't want to show it.

- Talk to your younger sister – she might be struggling and may need your help.

- Having a hole where your parents were before is difficult to fill. But if you need someone, then your siblings are almost certainly looking for the same support.

Find and confide in friends

- Talk to your friends and use them as a support. There will always be someone there.

- Find a solid group of friends that you can rely on, or confide in those you already have (for example, a boyfriend or family friend). Maybe some of them have been through it, too, and can offer advice.

- Make friends! If you need someone to talk to, then a friend or even just a regular peer would be happy to help, especially for someone in your position.

Talk to your mother and let her know how you are feeling

- Talk to your mother – I'm sure she won't mind listening. I'm sure she cares, but is just busy. So if you set a time for the two of you to talk, then that may help.

- Your mother would probably be more burdened knowing you were going through this alone. Don't vent to her all of the time, but let her know how you are feeling.

- It may be tough to bring up, but after you have talked, it will be a lot better – or she will understand more.

- Once you tell her how you are feeling, offer to listen to her or help her out when she is stressed.

Contact your father

- You should not completely shut out your dad – it is hard to believe he doesn't care.

- Of course your dad still cares about you – he's your dad! Give him a call!

Talk to your family – they still care!

- Slowly integrate a solid relationship with your family – it can be done! Call your dad, your sisters, your family – maintain a relationship, because at the end of the day, you can't choose your family: they're always there.

- Talk to others who are close to you and get support from them.

- I don't believe that your siblings/father do not care about your feelings – of course they do!

- Regardless of how far away you think your family is, they love you and always will, right now and in the long term.

Find support outside of your family

- In terms of talking to someone, how about a school counselor or a psychologist? Having a neutral person listen to your issues could provide a sense of relief and problems may clarify themselves.

PARENT Responses

Access support

- There must be a peer at school who can identify with what you are going through as a result of their own experiences with divorce.

- Find out who the counselors are at school. A counselor can support you and you can trust them to keep your discussions confidential and private.

- Ask a teacher or counselor at school to help you access a support group for teens of divorced parents.

Don't make assumptions about other people's feelings

- Ask yourself, "Who cares (about me)?" You need to talk to someone. You are loved and there is someone within your family/friendship circle who does care! So, find that special person and talk to him/her.

- What you are experiencing is real! It is difficult and there are people who can help you. Sharing and expressing your feelings will help – it will get easier and you will feel better.

Talk to other family members

- You are experiencing grief and feel the 'loss' of your father. Remember: You are *not* responsible for the relationship or lack of relationship with your father.

- Try and find someone within your family whom you feel comfortable with and confide in them about how you are feeling.

- Talk to your mom – perhaps she can support you in accessing your father. Your family needs to hear how you feel in order to recognize and understand the impact on you. If talking to them is too difficult, try writing a letter or sending an email to open the doors of communication.

PROFESSIONAL Responses

Ways to deal with grief and instill hope

- When things have bothered you in the past, what has helped you feel better?

- Grief is normal when you are faced with a loss such as divorce. It might be helpful for you to find out more about the grief process by searching the internet, doing research at the library, or talking to a counselor.

- What are the positive issues that your family can talk about? What do you enjoy doing with your family? What do you (and your family) miss (from when you were an in-tact family) and how can you fill that gap? Identifying answers to these questions can go a long way in helping you establish new memories within your family unit.

- Consider finding opportunities for your family to spend time together, such as special occasions or holidays. This may help the healing process.

- Find ways to reinforce relationships with others in school and within the family so as to help you find a footing as you move forward in the grieving process.

Identify a safe outlet to express feelings

- It's normal for you to feel as though nobody cares, but it is important for you to be able to say why you think this is the case. Is there someone you can talk to with whom you feel safe doing so? Can you write out your feelings in a journal?

- Consider joining an extracurricular activity to help funnel some of your feelings.

How to manage loneliness and isolation

- It is normal for you to feel like you don't want to burden others with your feelings or to feel like others don't care, but they probably do care and probably will not look at you coming to them as a burden.

- Try not to isolate yourself, as that could make it more difficult for you to work through your feelings.

Communicate

- You are assuming that your mother may not have time or energy to hear about what is bothering you. Are you sure about that? What would happen if you just told her a little bit about what is bothering you?

- You haven't seen your father in five months – is this your choice or his? Is it possible to talk to him about how you are feeling? Are you sure he does not care about you, or is that your perception because you aren't as close to him (physically, emotionally) as you are to your mother?

- What is the worst thing that could happen if you try to talk to your mother? Your father? Your siblings? What is the best thing that could happen if you try to talk to each of them? Chances are that the reality will fall somewhere in the middle.

- Is there anyone you would feel comfortable talking to about this? Who did you talk to about personal things before? If you can't talk to that person about this, is there someone else you can talk to?

- Try to stay close to your younger siblings. They may not know how to deal with the divorce either, and having you as a source of support may be more helpful than you know.

Seek options for support

- Check online or with your school to see if there are any support groups for children of divorced families. Divorce is very common, so it is possible that there is such a support nearby and/or online (i.e. chat rooms or message boards).

- Consider talking to your school counselor about your feelings so that you can have some support outside of the home. Think about having a family session with a counselor to talk about everyone's feelings related to the divorce.

- It might be helpful to have an objective person (e.g. school counselor) help you have a conversation with your mom. Consider doing so with the help of your school counselor or another trusted adult.

- Do you know other families of divorce? If so, how do you compare your situation to theirs? How do they cope?

What to do about self-blame

- What are your strengths? Can you use them to identify ways that you can talk to others about what is bothering you?

- If you feel that you are to blame, is there anything that you can do to rebuild the relationships that you have with each of your family members?

How to manage feelings of helplessness

- It is completely normal for you to feel alone and to not know how to process your feelings. The fact that you have reached out in this way (to this book) shows your strength.

- You have a lot on your plate and it's amazing how you have the strength inside to be sensitive to your mother's needs and, therefore, want to keep yourself from loading her with your problems.

- When you are feeling helpless, angry, or other emotions that come with grief, how do you express those feelings? Does that help you feel better?

Expat Teens say...

"Not seeing your extended family for months at a time makes it difficult to know what to talk about. They do not relate to your expat way of life, they do not know your friends, have not seen your house or school."

PERSONAL REFLECTIONS

"I'm terrified to tell my mum that I don't want her to work in the same school as me, because it's embarrassing and it gives me special treatment from teachers and peers alike, and I don't want or need that. It also doesn't let me do things I would like to do. For example, if my mum needs to talk to a teacher about a form or something, she will come into the class herself, and I don't get to talk to the teacher myself like other students. It makes me feel different, and all I want is some freedom and independence away from my mum."

PEER Responses

Talk to your mother and express how you feel about the situation

- Everyone needs space from family and many other things, so tell/ask her to give you a little space during school; having her walk into your class *would* be kind of annoying.

- Don't be scared about talking to her – she will probably understand when you tell her that you want to be like a normal school kid and not one with someone hanging over you.

- Tell her that you are not a child anymore and that you can take on your own responsibilities, like talking to your teacher about a form.

- Tough situation, but you need to tell her how you feel – be mature about it, as that will show her you're serious.

- You should tell her and explain to her why you don't want her to work in the same school. If she still does, then approach her and tell her to let you be independent and imagine/pretend that you don't go to the same school.

- How about writing down all of these reasons and presenting them to her? Make sure you don't portray them as too negative and say, honestly, how you feel. Having this list will show that you have really thought it through.

Work together on a solution, including setting boundaries

- There is most likely a mutual agreement with specific conditions that can be created (for example, not being in any of her classes, which the school probably forbids anyway).

- If your mum doesn't have a choice or an alternative, set up some realistic 'boundaries' (for example, you take care of issues within your classes by yourself) I'm sure if you explain things clearly, she will understand and form a good agreement/compromise.

Consider your mother's perspective

- Consider that she does not have an option to quit her job.

- Know that she would want you to express your feelings – she cares about you and will listen.

- If you feel embarrassed about your mum, trying to ignore any kind of taunts or jokes people might make is a good first step. Only afterwards should you approach your mother, because it would be a big change for her, not to mention upsetting, to hear that her child is embarrassed by her. Try to come to a rational agreement at that point.

Note/view this as a positive situation

- The way you feel is very normal!

- Think about and appreciate the benefits of having your mother at school. You will soon find out that having a parent that teaches at the same school is really useful.

PARENT Responses

Communicate with your mother

- This is a valid concern and it is important to open up and explain to your mother how you feel.

- You need to try and overcome your fear and speak to your mother about the impact of her role and how her behavior affects you. If you find this too difficult to do on your own, try to seek the support of another teacher or school counselor to act as a neutral, but supportive, party.

- You may be underestimating your mother's intent. She might think she is helping you out by the way she behaves in the school environment towards you. Don't hesitate to discuss how you feel. Give her the benefit of the doubt, as both a mother and a professional teacher, that she will be able to understand and see the situation from your perspective.

- This is a situation that needs to be tackled head on. You cannot, nor should you be expected to, 'hide' from your own feelings as a result of this situation, as it is understandably difficult. Your mother needs to be made aware of how her behavior is impacting you and your independence at school, and you need to be treated as an equal to your peers.

Talk to teachers or someone at school

- Who can you talk to and ask for support in communicating the impact of your mother's behavior as a teacher on you within the school environment? Can you talk to your father, another teacher, or a school counselor? You need someone to support you on addressing and working towards changing the situation to be more manageable for you and your mother.

Know that what you are feeling is normal!

- Your feelings are understandable. You are a growing teenager who needs privacy and freedom to develop your independence.

- There must be others in the same situation. Find out which other students and teachers are in the same situation and if they struggle with the same issues. Opening up and discussing this will enable you to learn different ways of how to deal with the difficult aspects of the situation.

PROFESSIONAL Responses

How to manage the struggle for independence

- Having a parent who works at your school can be embarrassing, particularly if you are older, as it may sometimes feel like they are watching your every move. Consider talking about this with your mom at home and letting her know that you want to have your independence at school.

- Do you have any other outlets for expressing/demonstrating your independence? Try to focus on those, because chances are, your mother is not going to change schools and neither are you, especially if you are in a place where your options are limited. So if you can find other ways to be yourself, then you will have something to look forward to.

- Wanting independence is a key aspect of adolescence. Talk with your mother about how important this is to you and see if she will be willing to do things differently. Try to negotiate the details with her and then follow up with each other a few weeks later to see how things are going.

- Part of being independent is proving that you are responsible. If you *consistently demonstrate* that you can be trusted to be responsible, then chances are your mother will back off a little bit and this will allow you some room to negotiate your expectations with her.

Communicate

- Have you already tried to talk to your mother about how you feel about this? What was her response? If you haven't talked to her about it, consider doing so, as she may not know exactly how this is affecting you.

- Consider role-playing with your mum so that she knows how it feels to be you in these situations and vice versa.

- Talk to your teachers directly and ask that they come to you if there is something you are missing or something that you forgot before they go to your mother. This takes a lot of maturity and guts, so be sure you are ready for this responsibility.

Negotiate/establish boundaries

- All students should be treated the same in the school setting, and school policy should be 'enforced' by the principal/staff – issues with students who have parents on staff should be handled in the same way as issues with students who don't have parents on staff. Therefore, if you are having difficulties with your mother crossing this boundary, it is completely appropriate for you to talk about this with someone of authority in your school setting and to get direction from that person about how to proceed.

- Talk with the principal or dean or head of year to ask about whether or not they can remind/reinforce the rules and boundaries in the school related to parent/teacher interactions.

- Talk to your mother about each of your perceptions of the teacher role versus the mother role, and come up with a way that you can be respectful of both in the school setting.

Learn to manage for the future

- How often do you see your mother in school? Negotiate with her about how much you see her and see if it is possible for you to have less interaction with her during the school day.

- Do you have any other issues with her outside of school as well, which makes her actions in school that much more difficult? If so, consider talking to the school counselor about a referral to someone outside of school, or talk to another trusted adult so that you can address those issues outside of school.

- Identify what you can and cannot change about the situation, and focus on what is within your control. Then, share this with your mother and find out which of those things she can control and find a way to meet in the middle.

Identify advantages

- Think about the advantages of having your mother at school, such as having access to money when you need it, getting rides to and from school, and so on.

Look for an advocate

- Identify someone in your school who could advocate for you and could talk to your mother on your behalf (or together with you) about how the two of you can co-exist in this school setting.

- Consider working out your concerns with the school counselor and invite your mother to at least one of those sessions.

Empower yourself to be proactive and acknowledge your feelings

- Consider finding other students in your class/school who also have parents working at the school. It may be helpful to befriend them so that you have someone to talk to who understands. You could even go one step further and create a support group for other students who are in the same situation.

- What embarrasses you about your mother talking to your teachers? Is there a way that you can prevent this from happening by taking more proactive steps yourself?

Expat Teens say...

"Being an Expat Teen is like not knowing who your parents are."

PERSONAL REFLECTIONS

'A family apart'

"I'm an Expat Teen and my parents are separated. I live with my mom, but my dad lives only a few minutes' drive from our house. My dad has an illness that makes our relationship challenging and sometimes difficult. He is taking medication for it, but it makes him blur and we can't communicate well. As a result of the separation, I have a very strong relationship with my mom, and I can tell her anything. Since I have no siblings, and I don't talk about many personal issues with my dad, I try to talk to my extended family. However, they live in another country and don't know the details of my day-to-day life, so they don't always 'get it'. I wish there were more people to talk to when I feel pressured or upset."

PEER Responses

Tap into friends and professionals you can confide in

- Stay strong and carry on. Find a professional who you can talk to. There must be a caring teacher or counselor at school who you can confide in and seek the support you need.

- Friends are often the best listeners. They might not have the answers or guided support you need, but they can listen and give you the time you need to talk to get things off your chest to just lighten the load a bit.

- Friends can be both a strong support and overly dramatic. Balance what you need from your friends with what you need from a professional; open up and seek more professional support.

- In terms of your dad's illness, talk to a counselor or psychologist – you need to understand the complexities of his illness and how that affects him before you can learn how to deal with it and understand what your role is in this relationship.

- Try to accept your dad's situation for what it is – it is neither his fault nor yours. You need to confide in someone – think about the people surrounding you who you trust and feel safe with. Remind yourself that you are not alone – many others have gone through or may still be going through similar situations and can offer support and advice.

Journal and find ways to get things off your chest/ talk to extended family

- Try to strengthen the communication and therefore bonds with your extended family. You need them and they are there for you; family is family.

- Keeping a journal will help you express intimately how you feel. This is a great way to clarify and confront your feelings and, therefore, better understand them.

- Think about the key people in your life: friends, extended family, your mum, your dad. Talk to them and confide in them. Someone will be able to offer the support and advice you need.

PARENT Responses

Communicate with your mother and others

- Keep talking to your mum, especially if you can trust her, because you both need each other.

- Appreciate the relationship you have with your mum and express how you feel about your dad. It is okay to acknowledge the difficulties and how you feel about the situation and the relationship with your father. As hard as it may sound, talk about how you feel about your dad. Getting it out in the open could provide a sense of relief, as well as create the opportunity you need to receive support.

- Talking to a professional, a school counselor, teacher or school psychologist is advisable. Peers at your age may be able to discuss one of your two difficult issues, but few will be able to discuss both. Seek some professional support.

- Reach out to your extended family and let them know that you need their advice and support in this situation. Email them, telephone them, and/or write them a letter to express what you are going through and how you feel about it.

- This is a situation that makes being an Expat Teen very difficult, as you feel your world is very, very small and it is often difficult to find that one person to talk to and confide in.

- Explain to the person you choose to confide in that you need advice from time to time and ask if they would be willing to listen and talk. Try to be very specific when formulating your needs and your questions.

Work on developing a relationship with your father

- You recognize your need for a relationship with your father, and perhaps he does too. Take the first step and contact him. Try and communicate your needs and decide together how you can work to meet those needs.

- Continue to visit and spend time with your father. Do not feel guilty about his illness or your parents' separation, because these things are out of your control. Share with your father as much as you feel comfortable sharing. Trust and follow your instincts when with him in terms of knowing what to communicate and share

- Find new ways to interact with your father. Often, doing things together, such as engaging in an activity or shared experience, is easier than sitting around feeling like you must talk. Sometimes talking doesn't work or is not want you want or need. Spending quality time doing other things with your father will make it easier to stay linked and bonded together.

Understand his illness

- Get more information and educate yourself about the details of your father's illness. This could be a great first step in learning how to build a new relationship with him.

- It is both sad and difficult to have a parent with an illness. You are dealing with two difficult issues: separation and illness. Both are extremely difficult to know how to deal with and to talk about. Online resources, support, and information could help you realize that you are not alone.

PROFESSIONAL Responses

Maintain family relationships/talk to family members

- It's wonderful that you have such a close relationship with your mother. Continue to build upon that, as she seems to be your biggest source of support.

- Even though they may not 'get it', consider talking to your extended family about what you are going through and see if they have any suggestions about what you can do. Even if they don't understand your life as an Expat Teen, they may be able to relate to your feelings of grief and loss.

Talk to other trusted adults

- Are there other adults you also feel close to that do live where you are and can understand your situation? Sometimes a caring and trustworthy teacher, coach, neighbor, pastor (or priest, rabbi, etc.), guidance counselor, or school psychologist is on hand to be a good listener. We understand that, even though you are close to your mum, sometimes you may want to share yourself with others so that you can get a different opinion, especially from someone who is not close to your family's situation.

- All teens need to have that one person they feel they can talk to without being judged, who can hold them accountable and who can offer advice when it is asked for. Think through all the possible people in your life (clubs, religious affiliations, social circles, sports, school, friends, parents of friends) to determine if there is anyone who might fit the bill.

Find other sources of support

- There are generally other individuals your age who have experienced or are currently experiencing at least one of the situations that you described. Consider asking the counselor at school if there are any other students you can talk to about these issues. Seek them out individually, or consider forming a group where all of you can share your experiences and share ways to appropriately manage those thoughts and feelings.

- Talk to your friends about what is going on and/or ask them to help you plan activities to get your mind off the situation at home. You may just need a break from everything from time to time, and who better to help you plan something fun to do than your friends?

- Feeling 'pressured' or 'upset' and going to the wrong person or persons for comfort or advice could lead to devastating circumstances. Try to make good decisions about this.

Consider seeking professional help

- Consider seeing a counselor or therapist, either with or without your mother.

- Talking to a medical or mental health professional could help you gain more clarity about your father's illness and could also give you suggestions and information about how to best relate to and/ or interact with him. This will help you to feel less inadequate or isolated.

Expat Teens say...

"I find it very difficult to constantly say goodbye. Teachers, friends, people you know are always leaving... people and relationships seem to be temporary in expat life."

PERSONAL REFLECTIONS

'Role reversal'

"I find myself in the more unusual situation of having a providing mother, not father. With my father at work in another country, my mom is working here, in the country we (my siblings and I) live in. I do not really talk to my mom about serious matters, as I do not feel comfortable doing so. I feel she has her strong opinions and would not understand me. Our relationship might be affected by her being an Expat and working and the situation we are in as a family. Nonetheless, I would not know an adult I could talk to. Because my extended family does not live here, my bonds with them are not super tight. School support would be possible, but I would not feel comfortable talking about some issues at school, which is normal for any teenager."

PEER Responses

Work on your relationship with your mother

- Try talking to your mom regardless of how you think she will respond. You may be underestimating her. Although she comes across as having a strong will, she may have a strong desire to make things work and is probably trying her best. Confide in her.

- Try to express to your mum how you feel. If you are constructive and not accusatory or overly emotional, this could open up a conversation and could have a positive impact on your relationship, especially if you figure out why you feel like you can't approach her.

- Talking to your mum about her 'strong opinions' may make her realize how she comes across, something she may be oblivious to. Work together on strengthening your relationship and ability to openly communicate. There is nothing wrong with you taking that initiative.

Seek anonymous help

- There are professionals at your school who can help. Often the first step is the most difficult one. Once you take that first step, it will make the next ones a lot easier.

- Try to find a way to talk to or write to a school counselor anonymously.

Talk to others (family, friends)

- Contact your dad and talk to him – let him know that you need him. Try and get close to him and further develop your relationship.

- How do your siblings feel? Talk to them – perhaps together you can open up to your mum regarding how you feel and how you are impacted by the situation.

- Share what you're going through with a close friend. Opening up and talking about what is going on will help you better understand how you feel about it.

PARENT Responses

Communicate with your mother and father

- Acknowledging the difficulties in your relationship and communication say you care!

- Tell your mother, if possible, how you feel. Explain that you feel that she is too busy to burden with your issues, but that you have issues you would like to be able to discuss. See what she says! You may be surprised at her reaction. Do the same with your dad.

- You're making some assumptions about your mother's reactions. Take the plunge – confide in her, tell her how you feel. Identify your needs and share them.

- Work on developing a new relationship with your father. He lives overseas, but is still accessible via email, Skype, and telephone. Confide in your father about how you feel and work on building something new together.

Reach out to someone

- Consider identifying an individual (teacher, counselor, extended family member) that you can contact to talk to about your concerns and/or to ask for help.

- Ask your school counselor or a teacher you feel close to about an Expat Teen group for people who have divorced parents or parents who are separated by geography, as some of the issues are similar. You all need each other to learn how to deal with this often traumatic life change.

- You are clearly feeling alone, like you have no family network. It is sad because it sounds like you are wondering – 'if your mother knew how you felt, would she be surprised or hurt?' Often, when parents are busy, children don't feel as loved or heard, or they feel like they can't 'trouble' or burden their parents. Always take the risk and ask. You are encouraged to talk to both of your parents and explain that you need more time from them.

Stay busy

- Distract yourself with hobbies, projects, and activities you enjoy, either at school or elsewhere. Do not spend all your time focusing on things that you cannot control or change quickly. Find things that you enjoy doing, and invest time in enjoying them. You need something to look forward to and to feel good about.

PROFESSIONAL Responses

Talk with your mother and father

- Try to sit down with your mother – you may be surprised at how understanding she is.

- Consider what it is about your mother that makes it hard for you to talk to her and get some suggestions from your father about how to best approach her. Consider having this conversation when both parents are in the same place (i.e. when he comes to visit or when you and your family go to visit him), as he may help to clarify any difficulties with communication.

- Maybe your mum would love to develop your relationship and make it tighter, which would allow you to converse more intimately. Try and encourage this by suggesting activities, such as going to see a movie together, going to dinner together, or joining a group (e.g. dance or exercise group) that both of you find enjoyable.

Seek support from other family members, friends, professionals

- Consider talking to your extended family — especially on your mother's side, as they may have insights into the best way to talk to your mother that others may not.

- If you have any older siblings, talk with them about how they would handle this situation, and if they are around, use them as support when you talk with your mother.

- If you have younger siblings, talk to them about what they are experiencing, as they may also feel as though they do not have anyone to talk to about this. If they know that you are experiencing the same thing, they may be comforted by that.

- Using friendship networks is also a great way to seek people's advice, especially if they are having similar experiences. They may provide you with an objective point of view.

- You said that the school setting is not an ideal place to try to talk about these concerns, but consider talking to the school counselor, or ask the counselor for a recommendation in the community (another mental health professional or a support group). Consider seeing that outside professional either alone or with your mother.

Expat Teens say...

"The hardest thing about going to a new school is getting on the school bus on the first day. The first day is not determined by the academic school calendar, it is determined by your father (or mother's) first day of work on the new assignment."

PERSONAL REFLECTIONS

PART 2

The Authors Respond

This section is a bit different from the one that you just read. In this section, we take a look at some more submissions, and we draw upon our experiences and expertise in working with Expat Teenagers to give you our feedback about how these situations could be addressed. In addition, we provide some resources and guides to assist you with your understanding of various topics. As with the previous section, we invite you to read through each submission, response, and corresponding intervention tool/data, and identify for yourself how you can relate and/or how you would help a fellow Expat Peer in a similar situation.

CHAPTER SIX:
Dealing with trauma

Sometimes, things happen and there is no obvious answer about how to deal with them. You may have experienced some trauma in your life that you are working through.

Trauma can be the result of an illness, death, accident, or divorce; an incident that is, in many cases, unexpected and extremely difficult to deal with because of the emotional, psychological, and sometimes physical, pain. If you are not working through your own trauma, then hopefully, the story below will give you the courage to do so. This is truly an example of how to overcome a painful event, one day at a time.

'One day at a time...'

"It was a Monday morning and I was going to school by taxi with my sister. When we were close to the school, we stopped at a red traffic light and there was a car in front of us. We knew that the taxi was supposed to turn right but all of a sudden, the driver went left and we didn't know why. All we knew was that he started to move into the wrong lane and did not slow down, and we crashed into a low wall. At this point I thought that I was going to die. We later found out that the taxi driver was going 40 km per hour when he approached the red traffic light, which caused him to 'fly' across three lanes, according to a young boy who witnessed the accident, before hitting the wall.

I remember there were a lot of people around the taxi straight after the accident. My sister and the taxi driver got directly out of the car, but I couldn't get out. Someone asked me the phone number of my dad, and they called him. I was in a lot of pain on my back and my stomach and I could hardly see because I had a big bump on my head that was bleeding, and it covered my eye. At that time, I did not know that I had a broken right wrist and left elbow, and internal bleeding inside my stomach. I also had four vertebrae broken. And I had lots of little cuts, especially on my arm and also on my head. So, I waited in the taxi and did not move. It took a long time for the ambulance to arrive and it was difficult for me to wait because I was in a lot of pain. A man and woman talked to me while I was waiting for the ambulance, which helped me not to think about the pain.

Soon after the ambulance arrived, my parents arrived, but I didn't see them a lot because I was put straight away in to the ambulance. When I got to the emergency room, I remember there were lots of people and my sister was next to me. My sister had little cuts and she didn't remember any of the accident. It is like it affected her memory. After the accident, she only had flashbacks of parts of the accident. She stayed in hospital for one week, and I stayed ten days: five days in intensive care, and then five days in high dependency, and then I went home. My mom and dad visited me and my sister every day, and sometimes they slept in the hospital. Lots of friends came to visit me, and even some of my family from my home country came to visit.

When I returned home I had to always wear the plaster and the corset and I had a bandage for the scar. It was annoying because I could not do sport for three months. I had to go to the hospital regularly so that the doctor could check me, but sometimes it was difficult to go in the car because I felt frightened. The two months in which I had to stay at home became annoying. I should have been at home only for a month but I was at home for two months because I could not take the bus – it was too scary for me and my dad could not take me to school because he was working. So my parents enrolled me into another school, which I could walk to, as it was very near.

At Christmas-time, my family and I could not go to our home country because of the accident – I had a fear of the plane, so we could not fly. I also became scared of lifts and all forms of transport. Also, I could not take transport unless my dad was there, but he works, so it was difficult to go anywhere. Sometimes, my friends came and visited me, and then I would go to visit the friends who lived near me. I had problems sleeping and I had a lot of nightmares. At the beginning, I could not walk for a long time in the street because I was scared of cars.

I realize that the accident had a big effect on me in that I had to have a long time off school, and then I had to change schools (twice). I experienced nightmares and flashbacks of the accident, and I became frightened of some things that I had not been frightened of before.

A year after the accident, I am able to travel in my dad's car and my friend's car, and I have traveled by public bus lots of times. I can now go to school on a public bus every day. I can go in the lift to my apartment easily every day, and in other lifts if going only one or two levels up. Sometimes, I remember the car accident, but now I rarely have nightmares.

In the future I would like to go in an aeroplane to leave the country where I'm currently living..."

Author Response

Trauma can be devastating to teenagers due to the direct impact that it can have on various aspects of self-concept. In this situation, the teenager described a rather horrific event, a difficult recovery, and a subsequent fear of things that she may not have ever feared at her age were it not for the accident (such as going on a bus and riding a lift). She also described issues related to her self-confidence, including the fact that she only felt safe with her father, and that it took her a long time to engage in some of the activities that she may have done without difficulty before the accident. As we have mentioned throughout this book, being a teenager can be difficult, but this phase of life can be even more difficult when you are an Expat Teenager. The level of family support that you may expect may not be readily accessible because of the fact that your primary caregiver (in this case, her father) travels a lot. In addition, it may not be feasible for you to recover as quickly as you would in a setting where you have 'all of the comforts of home'. However, this Expat Teen identified ways that she could cope, using the resources at her disposal.

The information listed below has been provided for you to use as a resource in the event that you experience trauma. This is not an exhaustive list, but rather a guide to help you identify the best way to move forward in the event that you experience trauma.

The following information, as taken from Helpguide.org (http://www.helpguide.org/mental/emotional_psychological_trauma.htm), can be used as a guideline for dealing with trauma…

A stressful event is most likely to be traumatic if:

- It happened unexpectedly.
- You were unprepared for it.
- You felt powerless to prevent it.
- It happened repeatedly.
- Someone was intentionally cruel.
- It happened in childhood.

Trauma self-help strategies

- **Don't isolate.** Following a trauma, you may want to withdraw from others. But isolation makes things worse. Connecting to others will help you heal, so make an effort to maintain your relationships and avoid spending too much time alone.

- **Ask for support.** It's important to talk about your feelings and ask for the help you need. Turn to a trusted family member, friend, counselor, or clergyman. You may also want to join a support group for trauma survivors. Support groups are especially helpful if your personal support network is limited.

- **Establish a daily routine.** In order to stay grounded after a trauma, it helps to have a structured schedule to follow. Try to stick to a daily routine, with regular times for waking, sleeping, eating, working, and exercise. Make sure to schedule time for relaxing and social activities, too.

- **Take care of your health.** A healthy body increases your ability to cope with stress. Get plenty of rest, exercise regularly, and eat a well-balanced diet. It's also important to avoid alcohol and drugs. Alcohol and drug use can worsen your trauma symptoms and exacerbate feelings of depression, anxiety, and isolation.

Expat Teens say…

"I sometimes have the feeling of wanting to 'go home', but I do not know where or what to call home."

PERSONAL REFLECTIONS

CHAPTER SEVEN:
What happens after Expat Teen life?

'The only life I know'

"Since I was three weeks old, I have been an Expat. There have been times when it has been hard and I have just wanted to curl up into a little ball in my bedroom and push out the world around me. Being an Expat Teen, I just cannot afford this socially. I constantly have to maintain my relationships with everybody, but sometimes I think, Is it really worth it? because I will probably move away at one point or another. I am originally from a different country than the one in which I currently live, but I do not feel like I'm from my home country in my heart. It really broke my heart to leave the last country in which I lived, as it was the one place where I felt at home. I wish every day that I could just go back and live my life there and actually be happy. There are a lot of problems with being an Expat Teen: adjusting to the school, the people, and your new surroundings. Most of the time, your grades will drop, you will have trouble making friends, and you will be upset that the new supermarket does not have your favorite kind of peanut butter. Usually, there are the same groups: the jocks, the 'populars', the druggies, the nerds, and the people that are just stuck in the middle. Also, drinking is a huge problem with teenagers, and some Expat Teens want to rebel against their parents, which can result in drinking and drugs. Being an Expat Teen is hard, but if you have a good support system from your parents and your friends, then you can get through it without any major issues."

Author Response

Developing and maintaining lasting relationships with people and having a 'sense of home' are two major themes with which Expat Teens struggle. When going through the adolescent years, which tend to be a long period of major changes (emotional change, developmental change, physical change, and hormonal change), it can be difficult to also have to deal with being confronted by the constant change of people in your environment. When moving from one country to another during the years of change, Expat Teens often miss and long for that one special person in their lives to whom they can bare their soul and share their inner thoughts, feelings and secrets, in order to help them better understand themselves. Despite the changes in modern technology and communication (Skype, Facebook, SMS, MMS, BBM...), these means of communication are not the same as being face-to-face with someone who you trust, and with whom you want to share time and experiences. When confronted by change, which is further compounded by the challenges of growing up, teenagers often go through periods of feeling alone in the world. It is in this Author's opinion that Parents, Teachers and other Professionals living and working with Expat Teens should remember the impact that change has on Expat Teens during these years. As such, we ask that you all strive to be more aware, sensitive and supportive as you help the Expat Teens around you navigate this phase of life.

Non-Expats tend to have many more 'constants' in their lives in terms of relationships and access to different people whom they can turn to in order to meet different needs throughout their lifespan. Expats, however, often do not have the simple luxury of time to develop the trusting, confident relationships with people in their new environment in order to be able to meet those same needs. We often do not take the time to think about our support system of people around us until we really need them, which is generally when we are in a situation that is too difficult to handle alone. The chart below outlines the differences in access to support systems in non-Expat environments and Expat environments.

Potentially Available
Outlets of Support for Teens

Non expat support system	*Expat teen support system*
• Nuclear family (parents/siblings/guardian)	• Nuclear family (parents/siblings/guardian)
• Extended family (grandparents/aunts/uncles/cousins)	• School friends (constantly changing as a result of transient lifestyle of expats)
• Neighbors	• Family friends (constantly changing as a result of transient lifestyle of expats)
• School friends (grow up together)	
• Best friend (grow up together)	• Church/religious affiliation support (changes from move to move, priest/leader changes from time to time)
• Family friends (known throughout life)	
• Church/religious affiliation support	• School (peer group changes from year to year)
• School (in neighborhood/community with neighborhood peers)	• School counselor (impersonal in a school of 3000, often have children in school which impacts individuals confidence and trust, approachable for personal issues???)
• School counselor	
• Teachers (known for years while in school system)	• Peer counsellors (difficult to confide in a peer, peers sometimes lack awareness and understanding of confidentiality agreements, what if peer counsellor has a connection-siblings, girlfriend/boyfriend, parents mutual friends- could make confiding in them too close for comfort Someimes there is a dislike of peer counsellor as an individual as a result of an experience)
• Community centres with volunteers and professional services, i.e. birth control centres, alcohol and substance abuse centres, verbal/physical and sexual abuse support, suicide support	
• Social services (public/free donations, private and government support/anonymous/available without parental consult)	
• Professional support (psychologist counselor)	• Teachers (often known for a maximum of two years)
• Helplines (anonymous)	

Expat Teens say…

"When home is wherever you live, you know you are an Expat."

"Moving around the world helps me to appreciate all the different cultures of the people I meet."

'Finding my voice'

"I love having the opportunity to live outside of my 'home country'! Every day I am exposed to things that others would never experience, things I perceive as normal that others would never imagine themselves doing. I am almost fluent in three languages – I am able to simultaneously write in one language, while speaking another language, and thinking in yet another language. It is sometimes difficult for others to comprehend, but it seems natural to me. Having been exposed to so many different cultures and viewpoints as a result of moving and living around the world, I feel I have become much more open-minded and aware of our world. I can easily see and feel this when I go back to my 'home country' and people there are all so alike. I find it weird and uncomfortable that the local culture of my 'home country' is so centred on being this one, perfect-type person, when I am used to being surrounded by so many different people! I know I do not fit in in the country I am supposedly from – I do not feel at home unless I am with my family, who is used to me and understands my differences. Others who I meet at work, or friends I casually meet, seem uninterested in my experiences and unwilling to listen, since I

am not supposed to be 'better' or 'different' than them. It is not like I am drastically different, but I clearly see differences in our thoughts and understanding of what we are exposed to. Their opinions are often similar, while I might have a new spin on things that does not seem 'normal' coming from someone of the same culture. Sometimes this can be overwhelming – school pressure, peer pressure, family pressure. How can I 'normalise' my life experiences and how they impact the way I see the world, and express myself accordingly?"

Author Response

The issues that you bring up are very much a reflection of the lives of many Expat Teens. Being aware of other cultures, having a 'worldly' perspective and opinion, trying to balance who you are in your 'home country' with who you are in other settings, and identifying what/where 'home' is, are all experienced (in one way or another) by many of your Expat Peers. As Expat Teens, you are not expected to have all of the answers all of the time, especially when the expectations for 'who you are' or 'how you should act' can change from one country to the next. In addition, the types of support and your access to that support change each time you move from one country to the next. It may be helpful for you to first of all acknowledge that your experience, while it is unique to those who have not lived an Expat life, is not unusual when compared to your Expat Peers. Learning to balance the issues that you mentioned will go a long way in helping you balance other aspects of life when you reach adulthood. It may be helpful for you to identify some basic, standard answers for some of the questions that you tend to get when you go to your 'home country', and also decide who you can share the more detailed responses with based on your perception of whether or not they will appreciate your experience for what it is/was. Be careful about assuming that the people in your 'home country' would not be interested in what you have to say or would not understand your experiences. It is possible that they are interested, but may not know how to express that interest without feeling like they are intruding or being nosy. Find a way to determine which of your friends and extended family may fall into the category of being genuinely interested in your experiences and then share those experiences with them.

When you start to become overwhelmed with the various pressures of life, reach out to your Expat friends and consider talking to your family. If neither of those is an option, there are several online chat rooms and blogs where Expat Youth discuss their experiences, and you may be able to have an outlet of support there. Chances are, any and all of these sources can give you some feedback about how to handle the pressure, as the people involved have had similar experiences.

Finally, find ways to nurture your 'unique traits'. If you are multilingual, find others who can help you continue to use those languages. If you have various 'ethnic' parts of town that may reflect one of the areas of the world where you lived, take some time to visit those parts and get to know the people there, as this is a way that you could continue to expand your knowledge base.

In all that you do, always remember that 'different' is not 'bad'! It can be intimidating to those who are not familiar with it, but if there is a way to make your interactions a learning experience for all involved, then try to take advantage of those opportunities.

Expat Teens say...

"Being an Expat Teen is bittersweet; you're exposed to so many amazing people and places, but there are very few others who really understand what you have experienced."

PERSONAL REFLECTIONS

CHAPTER EIGHT:
Alumni reflections

The best part about adolescence is the end! All young people look forward to becoming adults, and Expat Teenagers arc no different! Below are some submissions from Expat Teen Alumni – individuals who were Expat Teenagers and who have now moved into adulthood. Their experiences are probably very similar to yours, so it may bring you comfort to know that the issues you are dealing with have been around for a long time. However, these Alumni are proof that this, too, shall pass...

Looking Back: Alumni reflect on the pros and cons of Teenage Expat Life

'Adapting over the years'

"When you are an Expat, you either become very outgoing or build up walls to keep yourself safe from the hurt of leaving people. I was the latter. But I am older now and survived somehow. University was a great experience because I could share my worldly experiences with people that had never left the city they grew up in, and they helped me feel like I had a home because I was adopted into theirs. Email and MSN have been amazing. I was in high school before (well at the start of when) email became big, and that made communication with family and friends much harder. Kids today at least have it a bit easier."

'Fitting in'

"I grew up in a place so far away from home that our time zones were exactly 12 hours apart. I grew up with two really different cultures around me. It's a gift and a curse. On the bright side, I know a lot about both cultures and, as a result, I have love for the differences, and enjoy learning about others around the world. I have also made many friends along the way from different countries. On the down side, I never know enough to fully fit in, neither in the country I was born in, nor in the country where I grew up. I tried to feel at home, but with no success. It was not entirely my fault. People, I suppose, naturally dislike things and people that they don't know, and a certain stigma is attached to them. It's not their fault they are educated in such a manner. For me, the most notable gift this experience has given me is tolerance and acceptance for other cultures and people. I just wish others would accept me as well. I feel normal and happy on some days. Other days are just really painful. You get targeted – not physically, but mentally. They see you – the looks, the stares, the taunting and teasing. You feel alone because you're always the minority. My way of thinking is always different from those around me in both my home country and abroad."

'Understanding identity and developing a sense of belonging'

"Trying to decide where you fit in life and what direction you want to take (like in your career) is really hard. I still don't know and I'm almost ready to graduate college. The way other people identify me is a great challenge to me. I was born in one country and raised mostly in another country, but I maintained strong ties back to my home country throughout my life. However, I'm always behind on the latest music. I miss food depending on which country I'm in. I have to take a minute to adjust to money. In fact, I feel most at home in airports. But the truth is I'm isolated from my peers. Most people assume that my home country and the country in which I spent most of my life are similar, even the same. In actuality, they are not. Trying to be both

is really hard, and trying to explain experiences to people can be very frustrating. People don't believe it's all that different. I'm not the TCK that lived in Africa, went to school in Asia, went to university in Europe, and decided to work in South America. I'm the TCK who only speaks one language, but still has to know both versions, and who blends in with a crowd until I speak. Trying to decide what to do with my life is almost impossible until I work out who I really am.

I feel that, as a TCK, I need to do something really important and help other people, because I feel a connection to the whole world. At the same time, I feel like that forces me to have a really difficult life with lots of potential for failure and, along with that, the expectations of everyone around me are something I cannot or do not want to live up to. I frequently feel isolated. My younger brother just turned 18 and he is experiencing similar problems. There isn't really anyone among my peers who understands this situation. Oftentimes, I can get very lonely. When I try to explain the situation to non-TCK friends, they tell me I'm being stupid, feeling sorry for myself, or that I need to get over it. But lacking an identity isn't something anyone can just 'get over.' I also find that there's a lot of sentiment on internet sites that identifies being a TCK as all good and wonderful. The idea that I should be grateful for what I have (and for the record, I am very grateful) makes me feel guilty about also being lonely or sad. These are all conflicting things that I have to resolve within myself on a daily basis in order to move onward and forward. But I'm not alone. There are tens of thousands of TCKs, and when you find the right community of them (online, offline, or wherever), you can find a home for your heart and a place to really belong: everywhere and nowhere with your TCK brothers and sisters. And that's a really nice feeling. :)"

'Growth experience'

"I lived abroad my whole life, until I went back to my passport country at the age of 19 to study. I see my Expat experience as something extremely positive, and I am very happy with all of the experiences that I am so fortunate to have had. But everything also has a downside. One of the downsides that I experienced while being an Expat Kid was the fact that friendships were so short. Whenever I went back to my home country for the summer break, I would hang out with local kids who all had the same friends from when they were in kindergarten. That's when I realized that friendships were very different abroad. I never had a lack of friends, but friendships were just a lot shorter abroad. Whenever I would make a good friend, he would move away after a year or two. If it wasn't the friend who moved away, it was me.

On the bright side, I think it has made it very easy for me to meet new people and befriend them quickly. Another thing that I have noticed concerning friendships is the fact that I seem to get along with international people a lot better and develop friendships quicker with them than I do with people from my country of birth. I sometimes find it difficult to be myself when I am in my home country environment. I feel most comfortable among other Expats like me. This is something that I am very much aware of and is sometimes difficult to deal with. I am fully a member of my home country, which is where I'm currently living. But there are days where I do not feel home at all in this country. I think this is a problem that other Expat Teen Alumni must be dealing with as well."

*'I know I'm just 21, but I feel that my issues as a TCK began early on and got worse during my first year of college. I had a bout of depression, and it did not subside until I learned that I was a TCK. The book (*Third Culture Kids*) and the idea really saved me, but it also developed a complicated system in my head to navigate. Having words didn't make it any less difficult to navigate. Many of the challenges I face today are rooted in my late teens, and I feel like I'm not the only one dealing with such problems. College is a time to redefine yourself and to find your place in life, and being a TCK*

makes that particularly difficult. As such, I feel that, even though I'm technically out of the age range, I might have something to say that would count."

"I'm glad I'm 31 and that the learning period is over! Now, I'm an Expat Adult and I value my experiences greatly. I hope my kids get to learn as many things as I did!"

'Home?'

"I have made a lot of international friends here in my 'home' country, and it is when I am spending time with them that I feel most at 'home'. Getting used to a new environment takes time, but for some reason, I feel like it is taking more time for me to get used to my home country environment than it was to get used to the new environments I was constantly exposed to when I moved around as an Expat (e.g., multiple moves, changing schools). When I think about the future, I like to imagine myself moving around the world like I always did when I was a child. Even though I like living in my 'home' country at this time in my life, the thought of establishing myself here permanently is not one that pleases me a lot."

About the Authors

Dr. Lisa Pittman is a practicing psychologist who has worked in domestic (USA) and international settings. She is American, and her first international employment experience began in 2008 in Singapore, where she worked for a private practice. She conducts diagnostic assessments, and counsels International and Monocultural students and their families on a wide range of social, emotional, behavioural, and psychological issues. Her favourite activities include reading and traveling, and her favourite 'personal fun fact' is that she has traveled to all seven continents.

Diana Smit (M. Ed. Spec. Ed.) is the mother of three Expat Teens (ages 14, 15, 17) who only know Expat Life. Diana's teenagers have never lived in either of their passport countries (she is Canadian; her husband, Peter, is Dutch) and are truly global citizens. Diana and her family have lived in many countries, including Switzerland, Germany, Russia, Egypt, Indonesia and Singapore. Diana has pursued a fulfilling career as an educational therapist, and she supports the academic needs of International students as a result of their Specific Learning Difficulties.

Diana and her family have a passion for adventure travel. Their most recent trip took them to Churchill, a town alongside Hudson Bay. There, they had the incredible opportunity to kayak and snorkel with Beluga Whales, and to observe polar bears swimming in Hudson Bay from less than one metre away.

Diana's Acknowledgements

To my three wonderful Expat Teenagers – Hanna, Xander and Benjam – who only know Expat Life, as they have never lived in either of their passport countries. And to my dear husband, Peter, whose career introduced us to the life of being Expats more than 20 years ago.

As a family, we have had nine moves, lived in seven different countries, and traveled to over 37 countries. Hanna breaks the record of changing schools in our family, having attended a total of 12 different schools. We communicate as a family in three different languages, we hold two different passports, and all three kids agree that the most challenging question you can ask them is 'Where do you come from?' They have mastered both the short answer (one of the two countries from which they hold a passport) and the long answer – where I live now, where I have lived, and passports I hold. The answer they choose to share depends on the interest level and context in which the person asks.

Despite all the change and adaptation our teens have had to endure throughout their lives, they are all well-balanced, high achieving, fun teenagers who are going through the 'normal' phases of adolescence. They have made comments from time to time about how different our lives would be if we were not Expats, and sometimes talk about wanting to experience life in a Monocultural environment and experience being part of a community that does not endure constant change… but they quickly conclude that they like their lives and feel that they might get bored with what they perceive as a routine, predictable life in one place. We all go through periods of life when we think the grass is greener on the other side.

As a parent of three Expat Teens who has lived and traveled across the globe in the past 22 years, I can confidently say that I would do it all over again knowing what I know now. I think, as a family, we have a wonderful life that gives us access to a multitude of different cultures, languages, people, food, climates and many other things you cannot read about in a book or learn in a classroom. Exposure to travel and having different life experiences in countries other than your own are an education in themselves. You learn a lot about yourself, about the people around you, and about life.

Living a transient life through the adolescent years is not always easy. Expat Teens are often not in one place long enough to have a 'best friend', a mentor, or a confidant – that one special person that you know you can go to and bare your inner thoughts and feelings to because you share that bond and trust that allows you to do so. Growing up as an Expat Teen and being confronted by more change than stability and constants in one's life is a challenge.

Dr. Lisa's Acknowledgements

My journey as an Expat began as an adult, so in some respects, I'm a 'newbie' to the Expat World. As a result, I had quite a learning curve with regard to figuring out what this 'Expat Life' was all about. In meeting people like Diana and interacting with her Expat Teenagers, I was fully able to begin to understand what life is like when you grow up outside of your country of birth and/or country of passport, and it made me look at my 'Monocultural' upbringing in a whole new light. I am very glad to have been brought up in 'one culture', as even within that culture, there were many subcultures. However, my experience as an Expat has broadened my horizons that much more and none of it would have been possible without my family. So, I want to thank my parents, who were responsible for planting this 'travelling bug' that I now have, and for expecting nothing but the best in all that I strove to do. It is because of them that I am where I am today. I also want to thank my sisters, who have always supported me in everything that I have done, as well as my extended family and friends, who have provided me support in ways that nobody else could.

Testimonials

'Thanks for doing this! I know it will help many expat teens or simply provide an interesting read for us to see other experiences and lives like our own.'

Anonymous, taken from Expat Teens Talk *submission form*

'First of all, thank you very much for your initiative in starting this project! I look forward to reading the final product. Based on my own experience of attending middle and high school at an international school in my passport country (I lived overseas until age 11 and then repatriated), there is also an element of privilege that plays into an Expat Teen's experiences. Expat Teens are privileged and, in many cases, become friends with privileged locals, and this will shape the way they perceive and process common teenage experiences, including vices, sex, and engaging in underage behavior. There may be a need to differentiate experiences due to privilege from experiences that are in the domain of being an Expat Teen. Just some thoughts. Keep up the good work!'

Anonymous, taken from Expat Teens Talk *submission form*

'This project is a team effort and for this reason, it's got to be good. When I saw the title of this project, I immediately wanted 'in'. Having raised four sons, my wife and I have gained the experience and seen the benefits of a team effort. We encouraged our boys to always include their friends in our conversations, and we talked with other parents and colleagues, and guess what? It wasn't too surprising to find that when all their responses to issues were collated, they were not too unlike ours!

This project is a fantastic resource for teens, parents and other professionals to look at issues from everyone else's perspective, and it was a fantastic opportunity for everyone to have some input and a positive impact on teen welfare. It may not give THE answer to every problem, but it certainly gives a solid pathway to consider for each issue. Another benefit of this project is that it raises issues – it demystifies them, it lets everyone know that these problems exist for a lot of teens; problems are not unique to just one. And what's really good is that you don't need a long lecture response – it's a go-to book and you only need to refer to the problem directly at hand to get simple and short responses – and sound advice. I know this book will make a difference. Well done, Lisa and Diana! Thank you for caring passionately about teens and for making a positive difference!'

Buino Vink, Head of Senior School,
Australian International School, Singapore

'Lisa and Diana have carried out a lot of research to find some answers or at least starting points for many concerns of our Third Culture Kid students. This book is informative with multiple perspectives and the lay-out is easy to read, making it a very useful book for anyone in an international school community.'

Ted Cowan, High School Principal,
Canadian International School, Singapore

Expat Teens share positive experiences

"I'm enjoying life as an Expat Teen. It's a great way of gaining new experiences, learning about new cultures, and making new friends. I love my current school, especially because it's really different from my old school. It's more flexible and the teachers are much more interesting. Even though I found it hard to leave my old friends behind, it's definitely a huge advantage for me to develop new relationships. I always hear people say that it's so hard adapting to the changes of a new city/country and trying to make new friends. But my advice to all of you Expat Teens out there is to just be positive. Let positive energy flow and that way you attract great people towards you. I'm enjoying my life right now. I'm happy!"

Anonymous, taken from Expat Teens Talk *submission form*

"A life can be changed in the blink of an eye and, being an Expat, one learns that pretty much straight from the first (of many) moves to a new place. Trouble is, we hardly ever realize it at the time, when it's happening. I quite admire the phrase 'Don't judge a book by its cover,' but as many times as this has been repeated to me, it still hasn't changed the blunt and completely prejudiced way I evaluate a person for the first time... When I started school after a move to a new country, I took note of the students in my new classroom. I noticed one girl, in particular, and thought I had her figured out. Boy, was I wrong! Within a short period of time, this girl, whom I had initially judged as being a spoiled brat, had more in common with me than I ever thought would be possible, *and* she invited me to her housewarming party that weekend! What more could I ask for?! Turns out (which I confessed to her later), she became (and still *is*) that friend I'd always admired and envied and longed for, like I'd seen in the American movies I used to watch: the best friend you can gossip with throughout the day, do everything with, share every intimate secret with, fight about the silliest things with... but, eventually, realize that she is, and forever will be, the one person in the world who will understand and love you better than anyone else you know. That, to me, has been the best part about being an Expat Teen."

Anonymous, taken from Expat Teens Talk *submission form*

Appendix

Terminology and Definitions

Teen/Teenager/Adolescent (These terms are interchangeable)

According to the Oxford Dictionary, adolescence is 'the period following the onset of puberty during which a young person develops from a child into an adult'. For the purposes of this book, we are referring to individuals aged 12 to 18. The word 'adolescence' elicits a variety of reactions. These can range from positive memories and a pleasant walk down memory lane, to complete refusal to think about what those eight or so years of their life entailed for them. For parents, this word conjures up feelings of trepidation, regardless of their own experiences during adolescence, particularly if they have children close to this stage of life. Regardless of one's experience, everyone recognizes what adolescence means, and most people – including young people who are about to embark on this journey – brace themselves for its impact.

Expatriate

This word is commonly known among international communities to refer to an individual who lives outside of his or her passport country and/or country of birth. The word 'expatriate' tends to have less of an impact on general society, primarily because a small percentage of the world's population falls into this category. However, there are many facets, aspects, and experiences of life that others take for granted that can be magnified in the life of an Expat. Adolescence is a phenomenon that is influenced by the ever-changing world of Expat Life.

Expat Teens

These are teens who live a transient expat life, moving from country to country and, as a result, are confronted by constant change. This is a term that has been discussed in great length, albeit generally from the viewpoint of parents and professionals. Rarely are the adolescents themselves given a formalized forum in which to express their concerns and provide support for each other as they navigate through what could arguably be considered one of the toughest parts of their life – in what could also arguably be considered one of the toughest ways to live.

Expat Teen Alumni

This term refers to individuals who were Expatriates during their adolescent years and are now adults.

Third Culture Kid (TCK)

Pollock and Van Reken (2009) use this term to define a young person 'who has spent a significant part of his or her developmental years outside of the parents' culture'.

Profile of Peer, Parent and Professional feedback

The three groups chosen to respond were selected as a result of what they represent to Expat Teens, especially in light of the roles that they play and their experience as Expatriates themselves:

PEERS

Worldwide, the peer group of any teenager is a major influence. Teens need to know what their peers think and how they would act/ react and respond.

Expat PEERS

Expat Peers who responded were carefully selected to ensure a balanced sample of international representatives. Feedback sessions were conducted, during which peers listened to submissions read aloud, and then were asked to respond in written form in a way that they would respond to a friend, someone they truly care about and want to help and support. These responses were discussed as a group, and their feedback was collected. The group of respondents (all of whom were Expat Teens) included:

- Expat Teens who volunteer as 'peer counselors' as supported and mentored by their school counseling staff;
- Expat Teens studying psychology;
- Expat Teens of mixed nationalities, religion, cultural backgrounds, family backgrounds (only child, with siblings, placement in family);
- Expat Teens with varied backgrounds in relation to number of moves internationally and countries in which they have lived.

PARENTS

Not every teenager, or Expat Teen, has an open communicative relationship with their parents; however, they still need a parent's perspective on how to deal with issues that can be difficult and challenging.

Expat PARENTS

Expat Parents were selected to ensure a balanced sample of international representatives. All attending parents showed a compassionate understanding for the need of this book, and were very committed and caring in their responses. They were asked to respond as though their own children were confiding in them. Parent respondents (all of whom were Expat Parents) included:

- Parents of mixed nationalities, religions, socioeconomic backgrounds, education;
- Parents with differing number of teens/children in their respective families;
- Parents with different expat experiences and number of expat postings or numbers of years abroad; all have diverse international experience, having lived in many countries around the world.

PROFESSIONALS

In many Expat environments, Expat Teens do not know who the professionals in their community are. They also, often, do not know when and how to access these professionals in order to share and discuss issues they are confused by or struggling with. Often, when an Expat Teen has an issue, question, or problem and is aware of who the professionals are, the financial costs involved prevent them from having the access and, therefore, the support that they need. Depression, trauma, relationship issues, adaptation difficulties, and addiction, are examples of real problems that many Expat Teens struggle with. The Professional responses offer invaluable advice, support, and suggestions on how to cope with the challenges and issues as shared by Expat Teens for publication.

Expat PROFESSIONALS

Expat Professionals were selected to ensure a balanced sample of international representatives. All professionals have international experience whether it be working and living abroad or working abroad but living in their home country. Professional respondents (all of whom were Expat Professionals) included:

- Expat professionals with varying roles (school principal/head of school; school counselor; community counselor; university expert);
- Expat professionals of mixed nationalities, religions, cultural/ socioeconomic backgrounds;
- Expat professionals with different types and number of expat postings, or number of years abroad.

Participants in all groups have a wealth of International/Expat experience, and responded according to their personal, professional, and family experiences as Expats.

In all three groups, candidates were invited to participate with the purpose of promoting diversity. We were careful to ensure that individuals would contribute a neutral yet varied perspective that would best meet the interests and needs of Expat Teens.

ALUMNI QUESTIONNAIRE
Responses

Below are some answers to the questionnaires that we sent out worldwide...

Do you miss your home country or any of the countries you have lived in as an Expat teen? If yes, why?

Yes. Going back there feels like going back home. You miss the little things: food, music, the way people speak, cultural norms or the different ways you speak.

What is the easiest part about being relocated to a new country?

I was young when it happened, so it was easy to adjust.

What is the most difficult part about being relocated to a new country?

Growing up in one country with parents and relatives of a different culture requires a balancing act. There were more rules, because I was expected to conform to two sets of cultural norms. In terms of basic knowledge, oftentimes things were blurry, and they still are. There are many things that are fundamental in both cultures that I still do not know or understand.

Do you feel that, as an Expat Teen, the circle of 'who you can discuss sensitive, difficult, or challenging things with' is more limiting than that of your non-Expat friends and family? If so, why?

Yes. I feel like admitting challenges, doubts, and fears I have makes me appear weak. I cannot speak to friends because they do not quite understand what it all means as they lack the experience of growing up between worlds. I can't speak to my parents because they gave up their lives back in my home country to come to this country and achieve things. So, to have fears or doubts or be unable to do things feels like I'm undermining their dreams and lessening all they tried to do for me. It feels like, as an immigrant, I'm not allowed to doubt or not meet the expectations of my current country.

No. Generally, my friends and I did a very good job of keeping in touch through letters and phone calls, so I always had a strong support group, no matter where I was.

When you were in high school or between the ages of 14–18, did you engage in or try any of the following? (If so, please record the age you had your first experience with the following.) [average ages listed below]

Drinking (14) Smoking (14) Cigarettes (14) Drugs (15) Sex (15)

Have you ever been in a situation as a result of a decision you made as an Expat Teen between the ages of 14–18 that you did not feel in control of? If yes, please explain.

I had a one-night stand in my freshman year (age 18) after my first boyfriend to 'get over him', and after the fact, I realized how much it freaked me out. I haven't done anything like it since. I dealt with the sex issue by confronting friends. I was very worried how I would be perceived, and I'm still consciously aware of each time I mess up. I still feel it is difficult to speak with my parents for the reasons

170

mentioned above. I do not regret my world outlook, but it is a very lonely existence, and many people cannot understand the difficulties of day-to-day life. I have considered returning to the country where I was born, but I don't know the first thing about living there now, as I was very young when we left, and I feel as though I would be more a stranger there than I am in the country where I currently live. Many people believe that the two countries are similar in culture, but the truth is that there are significant differences that simply cannot be reconciled. They're two distinct places and two distinct cultures. I am also almost ready to graduate college and still do not know what I want to do with my life. I feel tremendous pressure to make life count, but that also puts tremendous pressure on me to succeed. Failure cannot be an option, and therefore I'm always stressed and hesitant to make life choices. I am often lonely even now, and I actively seek out online TCK communities because I attend a college in a small town with a very homogenous campus population.

Mind Map

This mind map provides a visual-graphic outline of the complexities of the day-to-day life of a teenager (expat and otherwise). As Parents and Professionals, we often forget how complex and challenging the teenage years can be. This mind map aims to remind us of the challenges that teenagers have related to schooling, peer pressure, communication, and the internet.

The mind map aims to identify different areas of the lives of teenagers, including: difficult topics to talk about, international schools, internet, peer pressure and support needs. Each area has points outlining what teens are confronted by and have to deal with. The section Expat Teens aims to provide a visual of all potential challenges the Expat Teen is confronted by *in addition to* general challenges related to adolescence.

Mind Map Created and Designed by Diana Smit and Dr. Lisa Pittman

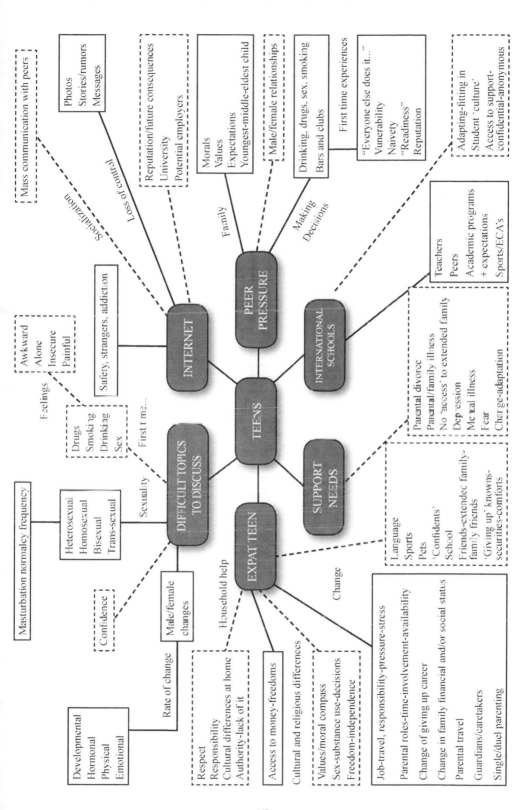

173

World Health Organization (WHO) statistics

In order to understand the needs of Expat Teenagers, let's have a look at the statistical data related to Teenagers globally. It is necessary to identify the various issues with which Teenagers, worldwide, are confronted. The following statistics, as taken from the World Health Organization website (www.who.int), provide a snapshot of some of the key issues confronting Teenagers around the world today:

STATS

(Taken from World Health Organization website)

- Teen Depression:

  - 1/5 of teens will have depression before age 18;
  - 20-50% of teens with depression have a family history of depression or other mental health problems;
  - 30% of those with depression also have substance abuse problems.
  - Teen Suicide: 2nd leading cause of death among teens 15-19 years old

- Teen Substance Abuse:
  - Teenagers turn to cigarettes and alcohol for the same reasons: curiosity, boredom, as a way to forget their problems;
  - Girls and boys may start drinking because of a lack of communication, support, and monitoring from parents.

- Teen Pregnancy and Sexuality:
  - One in every ten births worldwide is to a mother who is still a child herself;
  - Homosexual teens are more likely than their heterosexual counterparts to use alcohol or other drugs, engage in risky sexual behaviors, or run away from home.

- Teen STI's:
  - 1/5 of people living with HIV are living in Asia and infection rates are increasing quickly;
  - People aged 15-24 accounted for approx. 45% of new HIV infections worldwide in 2007.

The following statistics (which are based on an average) come from a collection of questionnaires as completed and submitted via our website, **www.expatteens.org**. During our research we reached out to schools, relocation agencies, multinational companies, and embassies worldwide. The origin of these completed questionnaires cannot be traced, as we assured every Expat Teen respondent complete anonymity.

Expat Teens have the most questions about:
(in descending order)

- General worries/concerns/fears
- Peers
- Sex
- Body changes
- Drinking Alcohol
- Clubbing
- Taking Drugs

Who is 'Today's Expat Teen'?

Out of 248 questionnaires we discovered 'Today's Expat Teen':

- Is 15 years old

- Has lived in 3 countries

- Has attended 4 schools

- Speaks 2 languages fluently

Experimental Behaviors Expat Teens engage in:
(in descending order)

- Drinking alcohol

- Illegal activities (obtaining a fake ID)

- Smoking cigarettes

- Entering night clubs/bars underage

- Having sex

- Taking drugs

Expat Teens worry most about:
(in descending order)

- Grades

- School

- Body changes (in relation to puberty)

- Peer pressure

- Boy/girl relationships

- Sports

What is easy/difficult about being relocated to a new country?

EASY	DIFFICULT
Getting on the plane (both easy and difficult)	Getting on the plane (both easy and difficult)
Nothing is 'easy' about moving to a new country	Growing up in one country and having family (cousins, aunts, uncles, etc) in another requires a balancing act of living between and knowing both
New adventures and opportunities	Having to learn about and adapt to new cultural norms and learn a new language
Having a "clean slate", making new friends, having a "new slate"	Saying good bye to friends, teachers, friends of the family
Unpacking	Staying in touch with those you left behind, people get busy and priorities change, you do 'lose' contact and therefore relationships
The 'Business Class' flight	Knowing where you really belong; fitting in
Most international schools have a changing student body and are pretty friendly to new students	Having to leave a place I grow attached to and start to feel at home in, leaving is so incredibly difficult
Packing and getting on the plane	Sense of loss, loss of a home, friends, school
A new house	Going to a new school, having to make new friends when social groups are already formed
	Adjusting to a new environment, language, food, culture, lifestyle
	Culture shock
	Everything
	New school, new teachers, different academic system and way of teaching
	Difficult to move from developed to developing world countries
	Knowing and understanding where 'home' is, it becomes less clear the more you move around or the longer you stay away from your 'home' country

Questionnaire example as completed for research and data collection

'BY EXPAT TEENS FOR EXPAT TEENS'

TEEN QUESTIONNAIRE: Just a few questions... please be open and honest when answering the questions below. If you are unsure, write 'unsure'. If you have more to share please turn this sheet over and share on the back. Thanks for your support!

A few details....

1. How long have you lived in your current country of residence?
   _____

2. Are you male or female? _____

3. How old are you? _____

4. How many different countries have you lived in? _____

5. How many countries were developed countries? _____

6. How many were developing? _____

7. What is the average length of time you have lived in each country?_____

8. Do you miss any of the countries you have lived in? yes___no___
   If yes, why? _____
   _____

9. What is the easiest part about being relocated to a new country?

10. What is the most difficult part about being relocated to a new country?_____
    _____

11. How many different schools have you attended? _____
    _____

12. How long have you attended your current school?_____
    _____

13. How many languages do you speak fluently?_____
    _____

What language(s) do you speak with your parents? _____
_____
With your siblings? _____
With your peers? _____

Personal and social details...

14. Do you have any teenage siblings that live at home with you?
    _____

15. Do you have a best friend?_____

    _____

16. If yes, is he/she in your current country of residence? _____

    _____
17. If no, where does your best friend live?_____

    _____

18. Are you close to your extended family? (circle appropriate
    answer)
    grandparent(s) yes/no
    aunt(s) yes/no
    uncle(s) yes/no
    cousin(s) yes/no

19. Do you eat breakfast and/or dinner with your family?
    If yes, how many times per week? breakfast___, dinner_____.
    If no, who do you eat meals with? _____

    _____
20. Which of the following topics do you discuss with your parents?
    school
    peers
    sports
    social related issues and decisions (like parties and going out)
    conflicts with friends
    peer pressure
    concerns about friends
    concerns about school
    concerns about sports/art/music
    fears
    expectations

21. How many nights a week do you go out with friends? _____
_____

22. Do you have a curfew? yes/no If yes, what time is it? _____
_____

23. How much allowance do get each week/month (please specify which)? _____

24. What do you spend money on? _____
_____

25. Do your parents track what you spend money on? _____
_____

26. Do you have a boyfriend/girlfriend?

27. Have you tried or engaged in:
    drinking
    smoking cigarettes
    drugs
    sex
    illegal activities (like obtaining and using a fake ID)
    entering a nightclub underage?

28. If you circled any of the above, have you ever been in a situation as a result of your decision that you did not feel in control of? yes/no
    If yes, please explain: _____
    _____
    _____

29. Do you worry about:
    your body size and shape
    body changes (in relation to puberty)
    peer pressure (fitting in, doing what others expect you to do, doing something against your principles or values)
    boy-girl relationships
    school
    grades
    sports?

30. Who do you talk to when you have a problem or if you are worried about something?_____
    _____

31. Who do you wish you could talk to about things you worry about? _____

_____

32. Do you feel that as an Expat Teen your circle of 'who you can discuss sensitive, difficult or challenging' things with is more limited than that of your non-Expat friends and or family? yes/no Why? ___

_____

33. For which of the following topics do you typically have the most questions? (select all that apply)
    - peers
    - drinking
    - drugs
    - clubbing
    - sex
    - body changes
    - worries/concerns/fears

34. How much time do you spend per day on the computer? For homework_____, for personal/social/fun surfing_____ (please write number of hours per day)

35. Do you have a computer in your bedroom?

36. What sites do you most often frequent for personal/social/fun/ surfing? _____

_____

_____

PLEASE REMEMBER that we have not asked you for your name, tutor group or contact details. All information shared will be kept confidential and will NOT be shared with parents or friends.

Thank you for taking the time to complete this questionnaire.
Email address: byexpatteens.forexpatteens@yahoo.com.sg.

References

- Tina Quick (2010). *The Global Nomad's Guide to University Transition.*
- David C. Pollock and Ruth E. Van Reken (2009). *Third Culture Kids – Growing up Among Worlds.* Intercultural Press.

Recommended reading

Heidi Sand-Hart (2010). *Home Keeps Moving.* McDougal Publishing Co.

Faith Eidse and Nina Sichel (Eds.). (2003). *Unrooted Childhoods.* Nicholas Brealey Publishing.

Julia Simens (2011). *Emotional Resilience and the Expat Child.* Summertime.

Ruth E. Van Reken (3rd edition 2011) *Letters Never Sent.* Summertime.

Lyn Worsley (2006). *The Resilience Doughnut: The Secret of Strong Kids.* Alpha Counselling Services.

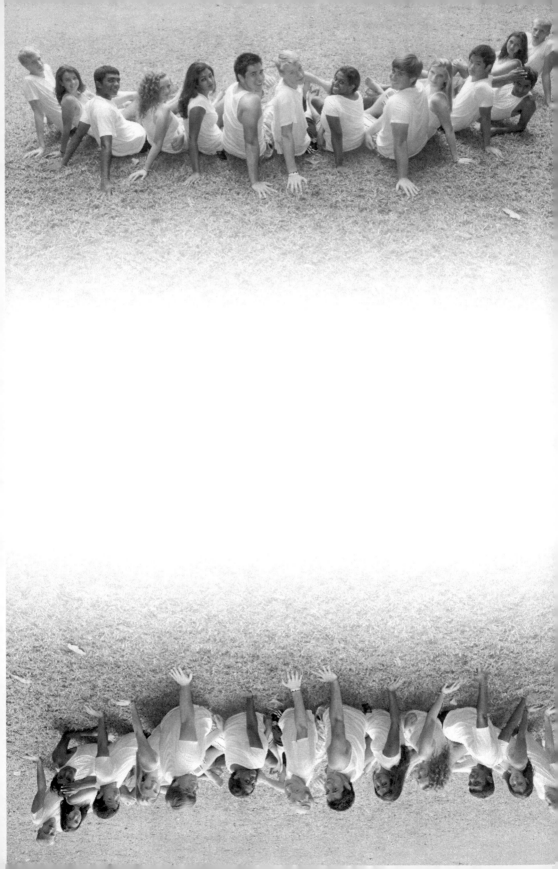

Lightning Source UK Ltd.
Milton Keynes UK
UKOW051950110612

194239UK00002B/84/P